The Art of War for Security Managers

The Art of War for
Security Managers

The Art of War for Security Managers

10 Steps to Enhancing Organizational Effectiveness

Scott A. Watson, CPP, CFE

ELSEVIER

AMSTERDAM • BOSTON • HEIDELBERG • LONDON
NEW YORK • OXFORD • PARIS • SAN DIEGO
SAN FRANCISCO • SINGAPORE • SYDNEY • TOKYO

SYNGRESS®

Syngress is an imprint of Elsevier

Signing Editor: Jennifer Soucy
Acquisitions Editor: Pamela Chester
Assistant Editor: Kelly Weaver
Project Manager: Jay Donahue
Cover Designer: Yvo Riezebos Design

Syngress is an imprint of Elsevier
30 Corporate Drive, Suite 400, Burlington, MA 01803, USA
Linacre House, Jordan Hill, Oxford OX2 8DP, UK

Sun Tzu quotations translated by Thomas Cleary, Samuel Griffith, and Ralph D. Sawyer.
Calligraphy by Dongxue Wang

 Recognizing the importance of preserving what has been written, Elsevier prints its books
on acid-free paper whenever possible.

Library of Congress Cataloging-in-Publication Data
Application submitted

British Library Cataloguing-in-Publication Data
A catalogue record for this book is available from the British Library.

ISBN: 978-0-7506-7985-5

For information on all security publications
visit our Web site at www.books.elsevier.com/security

Transferred to digital printing in 2009.

To my Lord and Savior Jesus Christ

"Some trust in chariots, and some in horses: but we will remember the name of the Lord our God"

Psalm 20:7 (KJV)

Table of Contents

Preface

I graduated from Long Island University in 1991 with a bachelor's degree in political science. In the years since, much of the specific material I learned has been forgotten in the whirlwind of family and career life. Even so, there are some important lessons I still recall. Dr. Donald Baker often told us undergraduate students that states are the product of both their history and geography. In other words, both experience and natural characteristics are to be taken into account when evaluating political decisions. As I look back upon my own life, this statement rings true not only for states but for individuals as well.

As a child I remember watching the news with my father. Like most young children, I wanted to watch cartoons, and I made this abundantly clear to my dad. Sensing an opportunity to teach me a life lesson about responsible citizenship, my father took the time to explain each news story to me in terms that I could grasp. Soon this became a regular activity, and, when combined with my dad's historically based bedtime stories and books, my interest in current events, history, and politics soon blossomed. While other kids were watching Captain Kangaroo, I was watching Good Morning America.

Today, people may argue about whether kids should be exposed to such material, but looking back, I find that my early interest in current events set me on a career path. The first news story I remember following on a daily basis was the kidnapping and subsequent murder of former Italian Premier Aldo Moro by the Red Brigades. Terrorism from across the sea was brought directly into my living room. Even at such a young age, my sense of fair play and knowledge of right and wrong was offended.

On a personal level, my young mind equated this type of international "bullying" with conflicts that I had with some of my classmates. Like many young boys, I found myself getting into fights with bullies on a fairly consistent basis. As a result of these various inputs into my developing character, I grew to not only hate injustice but to gain an understanding of human nature that outpaced my chronological age.

As I grew older, I saw the U.S. Embassy in Iran taken over and 50 Americans held hostage for 444 days. A relatively steady diet of airline hijackings and other terrorist incidents followed, so that by the time I went to graduate high school in 1986, I felt that my path was clearly laid out before me: I'd join the Marines and do my part to make the world a better place. What I didn't count on was a medical history that would alter my future; the Marines, then the Navy, Army, and Air Force all, in turn, said no to my attempts to enlist.

With all my other options spent, I decided to go off to school, and by 1991 I graduated, got married, and moved to Boston. As a 23-year-old with a bachelor's degree in political science, I didn't exactly have people knocking down my door to offer me a job. Like so many of my colleagues, I took my first job in security just to pay the bills.

Over the next 15 years, I worked my way up through various corporate security, risk management, and consulting positions. In each of these positions, I've found that an understanding of conflict is fundamental to an understanding of security disciplines and, indeed, of life itself.

Although the study of conflict is, by its very nature, a worldwide discipline, much of my thinking on the subject and, certainly, my introduction to *The Art of War* came from the study of Far Eastern cultures and martial arts. Over the course of my life, I've had the opportunity to study Go-Ju-Ryu, Tae Kwon Do, and Hapkido. All of these arts and others, when taught by responsible instructors, have a tendency to produce people who are successful not for their fighting ability, but for their ability to use their God-given energies in the most effective ways possible.

The book that follows is my interpretation of Sun Tzu's classic treatise on warfare, as it applies to today's professional security manager. It is an applied "interpretation" because even a cursory reading of the original work makes it clear that Sun Tzu was not writing about business but about actual warfare. Nonetheless, the concepts elucidated by *The Art of War* are applicable, within limits, to the study of conflict in general. While many management books have been written based on Sun Tzu's teachings, none of them has addressed the specific issues that security managers face on a day-to-day basis.

The following version of *The Art of War* is meant to serve as a guideline for today's professional security manager. Unlike many versions of this treatise, the present book does not interpret Sun Tzu's work line-by-line.

Instead, those concepts that are most relevant to the professional security manager are examined and placed into a contemporary context. Those readers searching for a scholarly work on Sun Tzu's life, teachings, and writings should review the bibliography at the end of this work.

It would be easy to interpret Sun Tzu's work, and by extension the current work, as a manual for doing anything, legal and illegal, ethical and unethical, to achieve one's objectives. The intent of this book, however, is just the opposite. If you are searching for such a book, then you should make another selection. By studying conflict and the methods by which skillful "generals" engage in battle, it is hoped that the security manager will acquire new "weapons" with which to successfully achieve his or her objectives within the limits of law, ethics, and morality.

Acknowledgments

I consider it a high honor to publicly thank the following people for their guidance throughout this project.

My Lord and Savior, Jesus Christ: without your perfect love I'd still be lost.

My wife Kathy: your exceptional patience and love inspire me to face the world each day.

My father, Hugh Watson: for his consistent encouragement throughout my life, as well as his renderings of the Mandarin characters found at the beginning of each chapter.

My mother: for her encouragement throughout my life.

Jennifer Soucy: who first recognized the potential of this project, as well as Pam Chester, Kelly Weaver, Jay Donahue, and Betty Pessagno, and the entire team at Elsevier for their exceptional professionalism, patience, and encouragement throughout the entire project.

Dr. Donald Baker: I still think about your political science lectures some 15 years after the fact.

Master Todd Miller, for his review of this book and his teaching of the martial way.

Linda Florence, CPP & Lou Tyska, CPP, for their review of this book and, more importantly, their example of what it means to be a true security professional.

The ASIS Crisis Management Council and especially Ken Brady, CPP and Donald Knox, CPP for your professional help and support.

All of my colleagues in the security, business continuity, risk management, safety, law enforcement, fire rescue, military and EMS professions. Your daily dedication to professionalism makes the world a better place. Never doubt that!

1 *Introduction to* The Art of War

For to win one hundred victories in one hundred battles is not the acme of
skill. To subdue the enemy without fighting is the acme of skill.
Sun Tzu

Executive Summary

The Art of War was written by the famed Chinese warrior-philosopher,
Sun Tzu, some 2500 years ago. Fittingly, Sun Tzu's original *Art of War* is a
masterpiece of efficiency. This relatively small volume outlines the strategic
precepts of war-fighting with such brevity and clarity that the work has
become part of the classic canon of military science. Nonetheless, the concepts elucidated in *The Art of War* are not limited to the realm of military
affairs. Over the years, numerous business writers and managers, as well as
politicians, civilian martial artists, and police personnel, have applied Sun
Tzu's principles to their own organizations with great success.

This chapter provides an overview of the original *The Art of War*, as well
as a preview of the concepts found in this current work. *The Art of War for
Security Managers* is applied to today's security professional and recommends
10 steps that will enhance organizational effectiveness:

The 10 steps are summarized as follows:

1. Continually develop and exercise leadership.

2. Accept that conflict is both inevitable and necessary.

3. Endeavor to understand your own behavior and that of your
   adversary.

4. Assess your situation.

5. Keep the mission in focus.

6. Strike when the odds of success are the best.

7. Be able to change positions quickly in order to gain the advantage.

8. Adapt to change.

9. Don't be predictable.

10. Continually collect, analyze, and apply information.

Today's Threat Environment

Today's security managers face a universe of risks and vulnerabilities. The events of the last few years have clearly shown how an individual or a small group can wreak havoc on the very institutions we have pledged to protect. The attacks of September 11, 2001, and March 11, 2004, taught us that our enemies are operationally sophisticated, well-funded, and that they possess a global reach. They prefer soft targets with high shock value and have been rewarded for their efforts with worldwide recognition and influence. Similarly, school shooters have shown us that one does not need to be highly trained to execute a devastating attack on our most precious natural resources. The Washington, D.C., snipers illustrated how two people could tie up several local police departments and federal agencies for weeks. The anthrax cases and countless numbers of subsequent white powder incidents taught us not only about the vulnerability of mailrooms to biological attack but about the vulnerability of our citizens to psychological terrorism.

Unfortunately, these issues are only the tip of the iceberg. Today's security professionals must still be prepared to deal with traditional security issues such as internal theft and fraud, robbery, workplace violence, domestic violence, stalking, extortion attempts, protesters, natural disasters, and computer crimes. Internally, the security manager must also compete with other departments for his or her share of the budget and other resources necessary to carry out the mission. Paradoxically, as the threats have increased, the resources necessary to prevent and respond to these incidents have not. As security managers, we must be prepared to deal with all of these issues, and we must be prepared to do so in a manner that is more dispassionate, calculating, and, yes, at times even more "ruthless" than that of our enemies.

While we are duty bound to pursue the war on crime, terrorism, and other forms of social disorder, we must start at the beginning. To do otherwise is to be diverted from an understanding of our most formidable adversaries. The security manager must recognize that the most dangerous enemies are those who dwell both within our own organizations and within us.

Enemy #1: Emotionalism

History is full of last-ditch stands against "impossible odds." While these often-dramatic accounts are widely hailed as testimonies of true leadership, they are, in fact, cautionary tales of ineptness. In the West, we seem to be particularly enamored of the lone hero who goes down fighting against impossible odds. We see this theme in movies, read about it in books, and, if we are truthful, we'll admit that we wonder how we would measure up in such a situation. This almost universal desire to be a hero is dangerous because it is most often based on raw emotion and ego. As with other desires based exclusively on emotionalism, the end results are ruined relationships, wasted resources, and destruction.

The fact is, leaders have a responsibility to make rational choices to maximize return on investment. While conflict is inevitable, it needn't be costly. Difficulties will arise in our personal and professional lives. National and international crises will continue to mount. We may not have control over when these challenges arise, but we do have control over how we respond to them. If we choose to take a thoughtful approach, we can attain victory while limiting losses. If we choose to be ruled by our emotions, we will be defeated and lose everything. Conflict is, therefore, to be accepted as part and parcel of life.

Enemy #2: The Environment

The operational environment in which we find ourselves is never completely within our control. As security managers, we must understand that we must simply accept and deal with certain things. Complaining doesn't help, and attempting to wish our problems away is a waste of resources. Operational factors beyond our control may include our current staffing and budget levels, business decisions made by senior management, and government mandates, to name a few.

Successful security managers will constantly assess the operational environment in which they find themselves. Elements of this environment will include the type of organization and its mission. Is the firm in the manufacturing business, banking industry, or high-tech electronics? As the saying goes, form follows function. The form of the organization will drive the operational environment.

What leadership style is expressed from the top down? Does the organization have tight command and control, or is there a more democratic form of governance present? Are employees free to make suggestions and take risks, or are these behaviors discouraged or punished?

How is the market behaving toward your industry? Are you in an economic slump where capital projects have been frozen and employees who leave aren't being replaced? Is business booming? Either of these extremes and everything in between will have an effect on whether the security manager can make his or her move immediately or be required to bide his or her time.

What about morale? Are employees generally happy to work at the firm, or is there resentment? For the security manager, employee resentment can especially be a significant problem. Finally, what about the organization's history? Every organization has a history, both official and unofficial. Does the history of your organization suggest a certain pattern to how problems are solved? What does this say to you as the security manager? All of these factors need to be addressed when reviewing the operational environment.

Enemy #3: Unrealistic Expectations of Oneself

Just as successful security managers must constantly assess the operational environment, so, too, must they assess themselves and their department. Unrealistic expectations can result in missed opportunities, unnecessary conflicts, and a loss of resources. Successful security managers will constantly assess how they and their department fit into the overall mission of the organization. They will inventory the amount and quality of the resources at their disposal. They will realistically assess their liabilities, determine who their natural allies are, and earnestly seek to gage how much influence they actually have within the organization. Brutal honesty is of paramount importance. The security manager who understands his or her capabilities and limitations will be better suited to make dispassionate decisions.

Enemy #4: Lack of Understanding

Security managers must endeavor to know their adversaries as well as they understand themselves and their department. Traditional adversaries of the security manager include criminals, hostile competitors, terrorists, and activists who seek to disrupt the day-to-day operations of the firm.

Beyond these traditional adversaries, the security manager also has internal adversaries. Internal adversaries may include unethical personnel who seek to cheat the company or violate company policies, unethical contractors who seek to defraud the firm, lax attitudes on the part of employees, supervisors, and even some members of management, and, of course, internal competitors seeking the same limited resources as the security department. While the specific tactics utilized to deal with each of these adversaries will differ considerably, the overall strategic concerns are remarkably similar.

Successful security managers will be those who successfully identify their adversaries. Once identified, security managers will assess the enemy's mission, resources, liabilities, and natural allies. In so doing, they should be able to ascertain potential areas of conflict before they arise and thus avoid areas where they and their department are weak and instead play to their strengths.

Enemy #5: Ineffective Organizational Structures

Weak organizational structures and overreliance on individuals is dangerous. The manager who allows efficiency to suffer in the name of a favorite structure will eventually see his or her department disintegrate into chaos. Similarly, placing one's faith in a lone superstar will often lead to disappointment. Superstars don't make superstar teams. Superstar teams are made up of individuals who work together for the greater good of the group. The successful security manager recognizes this and structures his or her department to reflect and support the overall mission of the organization.

This mission-oriented functionality ensures that managers can adapt to new situations quickly and bring the unified momentum of their team to the objective.

Enemy #6: Lack of Leadership

A team that lacks leadership is a team doomed to failure. Managers who are timid, disorganized, or unrealistic fail to inspire those under their command. This failure leads to inaction and confusion among the employees. On the other hand, managers who are forceful, lack compassion, or are unethical, breed resentment within their own department.

Successful security managers will set clear expectations because they know that employees generally do what is expected of them. They will set a clear vision of both the department's and overall organization's mission. Above all, successful managers will treat their employees with humane and ethical leadership. As a result, the team members will believe they have a stake in the system and will willingly follow the manager, even during times of crisis.

Enemy #7: Poor Timing

Poor timing can result in disaster. Security managers who fail to act on information in a timely manner or act too early are likely to either forfeit opportunities to prevent incidents or tip off their adversaries that they are ready to act. Either way results in losses for the organization as a whole. Successful security managers time their actions for a maximum return on investment.

Enemy #8: Poor Execution

Even if the timing is perfect, the security manager can fail to execute plans properly. Managers who are involved in constant overt struggles with internal or external adversaries will soon find themselves and their departments to be wasted of resources. As a general rule, it is better to keep the department's resources intact and spend sparingly than to draw a line in the sand and fight to the death.

Security managers who fail to heed this concept will find themselves a burden to the organization they have pledged to protect. Choosing one's battles is a far more judicious and effective use of resources.

Enemy #9: Predictability

The security department that continually does everything by a rote pattern allows its adversaries to gain an advantage. Successful security managers will ensure that their department changes patrol routes, times, audits, and procedures to throw off potential enemies. The more predictable an organization is, the more vulnerable it is to attack.

Enemy #10: Lack of Intelligence Capability

The lack of continual information about the intentions and actions of one's adversary can have disastrous consequences for an organization. Successful security managers will, within the confines of the law and ethical principles, seek information from open-source material, as well as cultivate relationships with people who can provide them with information to better protect their organization.

These 10 enemies have a profound effect on the success or failure of the security department and, indeed, the organization as a whole. Be that as it may, none of these enemies, or the issues they bring forth, are new. Sun Tzu, the renowned Chinese warrior-philosopher, recognized this point over 2500 years ago in his famous book *The Art of War*.

Who Was Sun Tzu?

Although there is a great deal of scholarly debate about when *The Art of War* was actually written and, in fact, whether Sun Tzu even existed, tradition holds that the text was written in approximately 500 B.C. Sun Tzu is said to have been a military genius who, after writing *The Art of War*, secured an audience with the king of Wu and was subsequently made a general. General Sun defeated the neighboring Kingdom of Ch'u, invaded another kingdom, and intimidated two other nearby rivals, thus securing Wu's political and economic interests in the region (Griffith).

Although comparatively little is known about Sun Tzu himself, his work is widely hailed as the simplest, yet most complete, text on the subject of warfare. B. H. Linddell Hart, a military genius in his own right, referring to *The Art of War*, stated that "in that one short book was embodied almost as much about the fundamentals of strategy and tactics as I had covered in more than twenty books" (Griffith). Endorsements like Hart's are not uncommon. In fact, military leaders throughout the world have adopted Sun Tzu's concepts to the application of contemporary warfare.

Applications of *The Art of War*

Beyond the realm of military affairs, the concepts set forth in *The Art of War* have been applied across a wide spectrum to include the disciplines of civilian martial arts, business, politics, and even interpersonal relationships.

Martial Arts and *The Art of War*

Those who have studied any type of martial art have already come into contact with Sun Tzu. The philosophy behind the myriad of martial arts is the effective utilization of power, energy, and resources. There's nothing mystical about the martial arts. If you've wondered how someone can break boards without getting hurt, you may be disappointed to learn that it's not a secret technique—it's physics. When a small point of concentrated force strikes a broad, thin item with enough power, it shatters. This is an effective utilization of power to achieve a specific objective, namely, the breaking of the board. Similarly, martial artists are often taught simple escape techniques from wrist grabs. Instead of trying to overcome the attacker's powerful grip where it is strongest, the martial artist is taught to break free from the weakest point, where the thumb and fingers meet.

In combat, the martial artist avoids the enemy's strength and instead seeks to strike vulnerable vital targets quickly without exposing himself to the same. The more successful martial artists will go a step further. He will see the potential for conflict brewing and diffuse it so diplomatically that he will achieve his own objectives while making his adversary think that he has won the conflict. The most successful martial artist will see trouble before it starts to form in the adversary's mind and steer the relationship in such a way as to avoid the potential for battle. In essence, the most successful martial artist will never know whether he can handle a "real" fight. This is the essence of effective power: victory without battle and achievement without loss.

Business and *The Art of War*

Sun Tzu's teachings have become a staple of business leaders throughout the world. Businesses today operate in an internationally competitive environment. Competitors must first ensure they have a high-quality product or service. They then must get the product or service to market both as quickly and inexpensively as possible. Add to these basic factors regulatory and legal issues, internal political struggles, public relations, and external competitors, and the comparisons to warfare are made clear.

History clearly shows that the civilian leadership of a nation must accept the fact that, over time, counflict is inevitable. The business leader must understand that in order to stay in business, competition is inevitable. Just as the general must assess the strengths and weaknesses of his country's own army versus that of the enemy, so must the business executive assess the strengths and weaknesses of his own firm versus that of the competition. The general must assess the terrain. The business executive must assess the market. The general must ensure that his army is ready to respond to the changing requirements of the battlefield. The business executive must ensure that his organization is responsive to the needs of the market. The general must lead in such a way as to inspire his soldiers to take chances. Similarly, the business executive must inspire his employees to think outside of the proverbial box. The general must be an expert at timing so that actions are focused in such a way as to gain maximum advantage. The business executive must time actions so as to gain the maximum return of investment. The skillful general engages the enemy when the odds are overwhelmingly in his favor. The skillful business executive directly engages the competition when he or she is powerful. The successful general knows that predictability leads to disaster and thus makes quick adaptations to confuse the enemy and seek the advantage. The successful business executive also understands that predictability leaves his or her firm wide open and thus does the unexpected at the right moment. Finally, the general understands that intelligence is the key to victory and thus deploys assets in such a way as to have continual information on the movements and intentions of the enemy. The business executive must also collect and analyze intelligence information to keep track of the competition.

Politics and *The Art of War*

The concepts of Sun Tzu can also be clearly seen played out in the arena of politics. In most areas of the world, political parties and movements operate in an environment where no one interest group can dominate the rest. As a result, coalitions are formed, platforms are negotiated, and joint resources are utilized to secure the most benefits for the coalition members. Even in the United States, where the political landscape is dominated by two major parties, the coalition form of government exists in that both parties have broad platforms brought about by negotiated settlement. These "umbrella" parties represent such a wide variety of interests that many foreign observers of U.S. politics have a difficult time grasping the differences between the major parties. Just as successful military officers must understand the precepts of war and business executives must understand the precepts of the market, so, too, successful political leaders must understand the precepts of political conflict. They must accurately and dispassionately assess their own strengths and weaknesses as well as those of their rivals. They must outmaneuver and outwit their adversary, striking at weak points from a position of strength. In essence, power is the heart of all politics. Those who use power effectively will keep it, and those who don't will find themselves on the sidelines without influence or recourse.

The Art of War for Security Managers

This book will address *The Art of War* from the perspective of the professional security manager. While the original work was divided into 13 chapters, this book, in 12 chapters, will cover a 10-step process by which today's security manager may apply the text to his or her own operating environment.

The 10 steps are as follows:

1. **Be a leader:** Provide moral, ethical, and humane leadership, so that those under your command will willingly choose to follow you.

2. **Accept the inevitability of conflict:** Know that conflict is inevitable in all areas of human endeavor; it is imperative to study and learn from it.

3. **Know yourself and know your enemy:** Be brutally honest with yourself; know your motivations, strengths, and weaknesses. Endeavor to know your enemy as completely as you know yourself, including motivations, strengths, and weaknesses.

4. **Conduct strategic assessments:** Foretell who will prevail 99 percent of the time.

5. **Remember what is really important:** Keep in mind that it's not about your glory; it's about victory.

6. **Engage the enemy:** Engage the enemy when the odds are overwhelmingly in your favor.

7. **Maneuver your army:** Make your organization swift and agile.

8. **Adapt to the battlefield:** Position your organization for victory.

9. **Avoid predictability:** Be aware that predictability leads to disaster; the key factor to achieving the objective is adapting and changing to circumstances in unforeseen ways.

10. **Collect intelligence:** Cultivate high-quality intelligence; it makes you better informed and lessens the need to do battle and thus waste resources.

In the chapters that follow, we will examine each of these concepts through the teachings of Sun Tzu and apply them to the security manager.

Discussion Questions

1. Does using the language and lessons of war to examine business make you more likely or less likely to engage in conflict?

2. Sun Tzu's *The Art of War* has been adapted and applied to many fields of human endeavor. As a security professional, what direct applications can you see between the study of warfare and the practice of security today?

3. Several enemies of the security professional were discussed earlier in the Chapter. Pick two of them and briefly describe how they could impact the overall success of your security department.

2 *Be a Leader!*

The Way means inducing the people to have the same aim as the leadership, so that they will share death and share life, without fear of danger.
Sun Tzu

Executive Summary

What is the role of a leader? What characteristics distinguish a good leader from a poor leader? Are there certain general rules for leadership? Are there certain traits that are dangerous in leaders? These questions and others like them are fundamental to understanding any organization, whether the organization is an army, a business, a department, or a nation.

This chapter asks the fundamental question of leadership.

Who Would You Follow into Battle?

To help the reader answer this question, let us examine leadership from Sun Tzu's perspective on warfare. Sun Tzu identified five characteristics of successful leadership and five common faults of leadership (Cleary). This chapter examines each one.

Five characteristics of successful leadership

- Intelligence
- Trustworthiness
- Humaneness
- Courage
- Sternness

Five common faults of leadership

- Recklessness
- Excessive caution
- Easily angered nature
- Oversensitivity
- Proneness to anxiety

Fundamental Questions

Who would you follow into battle? Think about it a moment. Out of everyone you know, professionally or personally, who engenders enough of your confidence and respect that you would willingly accompany them to face the strong possibility of a violent death? Better still, what characteristics would engender this level of confidence and respect?

Okay, so most of us have never seen combat and probably never will. The fundamental question still stands, albeit with some modifications. If the high-rise building is on fire, who do you follow to the stairwell and why? If a make-or-break business decision needs to be made, behind whom do you cast your support? When the doctor tells you to lose weight and start exercising, do you listen?

The answer to each of these questions carries with it potentially high-stake consequences. Following the wrong person into battle or down the wrong stairwell may quickly cost you your life. Supporting the wrong person in a business decision may get you fired, result in severe damage to your organization, or both. Not listening to the doctor may lead to an eventual incapacitation, bankruptcy, and death. The one thing each of these questions has in common is the question of leadership.

Who Should Lead and Why?

Throughout history many theories have been proposed about who was best suited for leadership. For most of history, kings claimed to rule by divine right and blood line. The rise of the nobles and middle classes gradually eroded this oligarchy and replaced it with the concept that society needed to be ruled by those with economic means. As societies became more complex, other theories arose. These theories compared the state to a ship and reasoned that if people were going on an ocean voyage, they wouldn't elect the most popular person to be captain; they would need an experienced seaman. Since government is even more dangerous than an ocean voyage, it is the experts, claimed the theorists, who should bear rule. Democratically minded individuals later argued, and still do, that individuals can collectively make decisions as to who should rule and why. Those with a bent toward anarchism as well as "pure" Marxists argue that government is not needed at all because people can rule themselves and still live in peace.

Wherever one falls on the political spectrum, the question of leadership is a key element in the success or failure of any organization. In warfare, leadership, or lack thereof, is of vital importance because each member of a unit must work together, not only to achieve military objectives, but to survive. In the business world this is also true. If the organization is divided as to its purpose and/or course of action, factions begin to develop. These factions will compete with one another and eventually weaken the organization to such a point that it hands its adversaries the gift of victory.

The Leader's Role and Characteristics

The leader's job, then, is to keep this problem and others like it from robbing the organization of its purpose, energy, and victory. Accomplishing this objective requires a set of characteristics that are not at all as common as contemporary society would have us believe.

Sun Tzu said, "Leadership is a matter of intelligence, trustworthiness, humaneness, courage and sternness" (Cleary) (p. 4).

Intelligence

The third edition of the *Random House Webster's Dictionary* defines intelligence as the "capacity for learning, reasoning, and understanding." These skills are just as critical to effective leadership today as they were in Sun Tzu's time.

Every organization has an operational environment with its own unique set of problems. Intelligence, in the colloquial sense, is a key element in both problem analysis and the development of an action plan. While a leader need not be an expert on every operational detail of the organization, he does need solid reasoning skills, as well as an understanding of each function and how it contributes to the overall mission of the organization.

Beyond analytical capabilities, intelligence serves to inspire the troops. As was asked at the beginning of the chapter; who would you follow into battle? Would you be likely to follow someone who seemed out of touch with the situation at hand? Would you be willing to follow someone who wasn't knowledgeable about combat? What if the leader's expectation of you wasn't clear? What if the mission was vague? Would that make you comfortable?

Security managers, like military officers and other leaders, must understand that those under their command **will** reason why. They **will** observe your every move, and they **will** make judgments about your competency. Whereas soldiers in modern armies have little recourse but to follow their officers, this is not true in the civilian world, where people can come and go with ease and where the chain of command is less clear-cut. Private-sector security managers who lack the requisite intelligence needed for their position will find themselves:

1. Unable to understand the operational environment
2. Unable to formulate a workable action plan
3. Unable to inspire their current staff
4. Unable to reduce high turnover rates and thereby field an experienced team
5. Unable to accomplish the mission
6. Unable to please their superiors
7. Unable to hold onto their position

The lessons here are clear:

1. Business leaders must take great pains to properly select, train, and manage those who will be responsible for protecting the firm's assets.
2. Security professionals must continually seek to learn new skills, polish old skills, and inspire their staffs.

Trustworthiness

Trust is the cornerstone of all successful relationships, whether married couples, platoons, football teams, or multibillion-dollar enterprises are involved. In the absence of trust, people tend to hold back information, they become suspicious of teammates, and they try to do everything themselves. The result of such a situation is an inefficient use of energy and eventual disintegration into chaos. When the staff doesn't trust the leader, this situation is compounded by subtle forms of resistance that undermine the leader's authority as well as the effectiveness of the organization.

So, what makes a leader trustworthy? Most people equate the word "trust" with personal integrity; however, the question is not as simplistic as saying that one leader is trustworthy and another leader is not. Rather, it is a question of what areas one is trustworthy in and to what degree. One leader may have a great deal of personal integrity but not be competent in a specific area. Another may be highly competent in a given area but have very little time with the organization. Depending on the criticality of the assignment, it may be wise to wait until the person's integrity can be better evaluated over time.

When evaluating the potential trustworthiness of a leader, it is prudent for management to ask the following types of questions:

1. Has the leader been with the organization for a sufficient amount of time to properly evaluate his loyalty?

2. Do the leader's statements consistently match her actions? If not, it will be difficult for the staff or other managers to ascertain where the person stands.

3. Does the leader take responsibility for both his actions and the sanctioned actions of his staff? If he is ready to hang a member of his staff for following his orders, morale will suffer.

4. Does the leader try to agree with everyone? If so, one may not be able to rely on her in times of adversity.

5. Is the leader trustworthy in his personal relationships? If not, he may not be trustworthy in his professional relationships either.

Humaneness

Leadership positions attract people with strong personalities, as is to be expected. To presume to lead others takes a certain amount of confidence. This confidence, if not counterbalanced with humility, can lead to arrogance. Arrogant leaders are quick to publicly point out their subordinate's mistakes and blame others for their own shortcomings. They don't listen to their staff's analysis, and they can't understand why someone would request time off for personal or family reasons. As a result of these behaviors, arrogant leaders reap what they sow. Eventually, terrible working conditions, high turnover, and poor morale lead to inefficiencies, which are noticed by upper level management. Unfortunately, by the time these efficiencies are noticed, the department and the organization have typically lost quality personnel as well as potential business opportunities.

When evaluating a potential leader, it is wise to look for the following humane traits:

1. **Morality:** Does the leader have a moral code that is beyond himself? If not, to whom does he really answer? Do you really want someone who would do ***anything*** to advance his career?

2. **Mission:** Does the leader understand that most people work not just to meet their material needs, but for a sense of purpose as well? If not, she will think that the answer to problems will always revolve around money and she'll miss the big picture.

3. **Compassion:** Does the leader show evidence of compassion to his employees? If not, how does he expect to keep high-quality employees?

4. **Credit:** Does the leader acknowledge the contributions of her staff? If not, count on everdecreasing levels of morale.

5. **Patience:** Does the leader show patience with employees, trying to privately correct performance issues? If not, he may breed resentment.

Courage

Courage is one of the most admired of human traits. A courageous act can take place in seconds or over the better part of a lifetime. It can involve risk of property, liberty, position, reputation, or even life. Whether the risk takes place on the battlefield or the boardroom, the church, the classroom, or the courtroom, one thing is certain—without courageous people nothing of importance would ever be accomplished.

Courage is especially important in leaders because they are charged with rallying those under their command to take risks in pursuit of excellence. Military history is filled with heroic leaders and armies. The following are but two examples.

The Spartans at Thermopylae

The battle of Thermopylae is one of the most famous battles of all time. In the year 480 B.C. the Persian army, under King Xerxes I, invaded the Hellenic world. The Greek city-states, realizing that only a united front stood a chance in the face of the immense Persian army, formed an alliance, under Sparta's King Leonidas, to beat back the invasion.

As the Persians approached the mountain pass at Thermopylae, King Xerxes sent messengers to Leonidas asking that he and his army join him against the other Greek city-states. In exchange for his cooperation, Xerxes offered Leonidas the opportunity to be king of Greece once the alliance was defeated. Leonidas refused and remarked, "If you understood what is honorable in life, you would avoid lusting after what belongs to others. For me it is better to die for Greece than to be the monarch of the people of my race"

(Plutarch, p. 170). Upon receiving this message, Xerxes again sent messengers, this time demanding that the Spartans surrender their weapons. Leonidas replied, "Come and take them" (Plutarch, p. 170).

Over the course of the next two days, Leonidas' small band of Spartan soldiers held back the Persian army, estimated by some scholars to have been 60 times larger. This delaying action slowed the Persian advance, thus buying time for the other city-states to make preparations that would eventually defeat the Persians (Cartledge, Plutarch).

The battle of Thermopylae is one of the few examples in history of a sacrificial last stand that had significant military value. While Thermopylae was a technical defeat for the Spartans, it was an exceptionally costly "victory" for the Persians.

Lessons

- **Leaders must understand what is supremely important:** Clearly, Leonidas understood that, unimpeded, the Persians would have likely sacked all of Greece. The Spartans' willingness to sacrifice so that the rest of the confederacy could eventually defeat the invaders was as much an act of cold calculation as it was an act of heroism and sacrifice. What is supremely important to your organization?

- **Leaders must exhibit courageous integrity:** If Leonidas had joined with the Persians, Thermopylae would have gone down in history as one of the greatest acts of treason of all time. Instead, Leonidas exhibited courageous integrity. Can you be bought?

- **Leaders must utilize their resources to the best of their ability:** Clearly, the Spartans' use of the mountain pass terrain offered them advantages that allowed them to significantly slow the advancing Persians. Are you effectively using the resources at your disposal?

- **Leaders must make a commitment to training:** The Spartans trained for war from the time they were infants. This commitment to training made them some of the most feared and skilled warriors of the ancient world. How important do you consider training?

Jackson at Manassas Junction

One of the early engagements of the American Civil War took place near the railroad junction in Manassas, Virginia. As Allen C. Redwood of the

55th Virginia Regiment, CSA, noted in his work, *Stonewall Jackson—Memory* (Rodenbough, 1983, p. 100).

> The supreme effort of the Federal commander was directed against the left army of Johnston and Beauregard and upon the open plateau surrounding the Henry House. The battle was raging furiously, and seemingly the Southern line at this point was on the verge of utter disaster, when the Carolinian, General Barnard E. Bee, rode from his shattered and wavering brigade over to where Jackson still held fast with his mountain men.
>
> "General," he said in tones of anguish, "they are beating us back."
>
> "No sir," was the grim reply, "We will give them the bayonet."
>
> Bee rode back and spoke to his brigade: "Look at Jackson there standing like a stone wall. Rally behind the Virginians!" and the front of the battle was restored. The rest is history. (p. 100)

Lessons

- **Courageous leaders make calm decisions under pressure:** The situation at Manassas Junction was looking bleak for the Confederates. As their line was about to disintegrate, Jackson could have let himself be overcome by emotions. Instead, he calmly assessed the situation and made the decision to stand. If Jackson had agreed with Bee's assessment and ordered a retreat, the Confederate line would have collapsed and the Union would have had its first major victory of the war. How do you respond under pressure?

- **Leaders must recognize and address signs of stress in their subordinates:** Bee was understandably concerned over the events taking place at the line. Jackson could have berated him for his suggestion that they were meeting defeat. Instead, he listened to Bee's concern and then calmly but firmly gave the order to stand. How do you handle stress and doubt from your staff?

- **Leaders must be courageous role models:** Jackson's decision and demeanor inspired not only his own troops, but Bee's as well. In fact, Bee's message to his troops about Jackson "standing like a stone wall" inspired the Confederate military as a whole and gave birth to the legend of "Stonewall Jackson." How do you model behavior for your staff?

- **Leaders must make the most of the orders they are given:** Although it would have been considered both insubordinate and dishonorable, Bee could have rode back to his troops and told them that Jackson was stubbornly choosing to stand and, as a result, they were all going to die. Instead, Bee followed orders, overcame his own fears, and used Jackson's resolve to inspire his own troops. How do you respond to lawful, hard orders that come from your superiors?

The stakes are vastly different in the corporate world than they are on the battlefield, of course, but corporate leaders must also exhibit courage. Courage in the corporate world can be expressed in the manager or employee who challenges the status quo with new ideas or the employee who says no to unethical or illegal behavior.

The security manager who purposefully seeks to develop courage within himself and his department will have significant advantages. When evaluating a potential leader, it is wise to look for the following courageous traits:

1. **Calmness:** The leader with true courage brings a sense of calm to any given situation. This calmness allows for clear thinking and rational action.

2. **Integrity:** Courageous leaders understand that integrity matters. They take responsibility for their actions and see clearly because they have a sense of purpose beyond themselves.

3. **Understanding:** Courageous leaders understand human frailties and seek to inspire those under their command so that they stretch themselves beyond their normal capabilities.

4. **Loyalty:** Courageous leaders earn the respect of their staff, which results in strong loyalty and enhanced organizational and individual effectiveness.

5. **Vitality:** Courageous leaders become vital to their organization.

Sternness

In an effort to maintain order, a leader must balance humaneness with sternness. If he does not, discipline will break down and the organization will slip into chaos. This is especially true when an element of excitement or danger is present. If a group is excited about a project but lacks focus, all of its energy will be sapped as people set about to accomplish tasks without any coordination. When this occurs, morale will wane, people will leave, and the project will fail. If there is an element of danger present and the group lacks focus, accidents will occur, people may get hurt, and the project will fail.

It is therefore of paramount importance that leaders maintain order because managers who cannot maintain order will lead their organization to failure. While some leaders may be more democratic and others more author-itarian, in the final analysis someone has to make difficult decisions for the good of the organization. Finding this balance is difficult for most people, but it is of vital importance to someone who would assume to lead others.

When evaluating a potential leader, it is wise to look for the following traits considering sternness:

1. **Clear expectations:** Good leaders have clear expectations and make those expectations known to their staff.

2. **Evaluation:** Good leaders continually evaluate their own and their staff's performance against the objectives of the department and organization.

3. **Confrontation:** Good leaders must not be afraid to confront people who are continually breaking rules, not communicating with others, or generally going about doing their own thing.

4. **Follow-through:** If a leader has repeatedly made good faith efforts to bring someone in line with the rest of the group and still cannot gain compliance, it is incumbent upon that leader to either encourage the person to leave the organization or, failing that, to terminate the individual.

5. **Calculation:** Terminating someone should not be an act of anger or hostility, but rather a calm, informed, and properly documented deci-sion for the good of the organization and, at times, the terminated employee as well.

Failures of Leadership

Sun Tzu identified five common failures of leadership (Michaelson, 2001).

1. **Recklessness:** Leaders who are reckless in battle are likely to ignore the potential for losses and thus deplete their resources faster than one who takes the time to rationally assess risks, vulnerabilities, and poten-tial impacts to their army. This is equally true in the business world. Reckless leaders will improvise to the point where they will lose much to gain little. This inefficient use of power and resources will result in poor performance and the eventual loss of the leader's position to someone more thoughtful.

2. **Excessive caution:** A leader who is overly cautious has the exact oppo-site downfall of the reckless leader. The overly cautious leader will not engage the enemy. Similarly, in the business world the overly cautious

leader takes very few chances. While this type of leader may have a long tenure at many organizations, he or she will accomplish little.

3. **Easily angered nature:** On the battlefield, leaders who are easily angered are likely to lead their troops to death. In the corporate world, leaders who are easily angered allow their emotions to control their actions and either take reckless chances or fail to support other leaders in the same organization. The end result is depletion of resources for little gain, which in turn leads to them being relieved of their command.

4. **Oversensitivity:** Oversensitivity is a form of arrogance. Leaders who are overly sensitive think that the organization revolves around themselves and are insulted by the slightest disagreement from colleagues or correction from superiors. As a result of this world-view, overly sensitive leaders will passively resist the orders of superiors and sabotage efforts of colleagues who, in the leaders' imagination, have insulted them. On the battlefield, this will lead to a needless waste of lives; in the business world, it will lead to division and infighting. In the end, such leaders will lose their position, but not before causing significant damage to the organization.

5. **Proneness to anxiety:** Anxious leaders make the best decisions they can but spend an inordinate amount of time worrying about the results. This worrying is a waste of energy that clouds the leaders' judgment about newly developing situations. Anxiety-prone leaders can lose their focus, whether on the battlefield or in the boardroom. As a result of this anxiety, they become ineffective and the organization eventually replaces them with more confident leaders.

Leadership

We started this chapter out with a fundamental question about leadership: "Who would you follow into battle?" As the reader might imagine, my list is rather short. When assessing leadership, either in yourself or in someone else, ask yourself about each of the characteristics identified by Sun Tzu:

1. Does the leader have the requisite intelligence or reasoning capability to accomplish the mission at hand?

2. Is the leader trustworthy, in terms of both skill and personal integrity?

3. Does the leader inspire people?

4. Does the leader treat subordinates with respect and fairness?

5. Does the leader have the type of courage necessary for the mission at hand?

6. Does the leader know how to keep order and be stern when needed?

7. Is the leader's courage balanced by intelligence?

8. Is the leader's humaneness balanced by sternness?

9. Is the leader reckless, easily angered, or overly sensitive?

10. Is the leader anxious or overly cautious?

Remember that not all people make good leaders and not all people want to be leaders. If you desire to lead others, seek to be the person you would follow into battle.

Discussion Questions

1. Who do you know personally or professionally that you would willingly follow into battle or another life-and-death situation, and why?

2. Based on Sun Tzu's view of leadership, are you a good leader? Why or why not?

   Intelligence

   Trustworthiness

   Humaneness

   Courage

   Sternness

3. You've just been elected president of the United States. Who would be part of your cabinet and why?

4. Which of Sun Tzu's defined leadership flaws do you view as the most potentially damaging to your department or organization?

   Recklessness

   Excessive caution

   Easily angered nature

   Oversensitivity

   Proneness to anxiety

5. What leader, living or dead, do you most admire and why?

矛盾衝突

3 *Accept the Inevitability of Conflict*

Warfare is the greatest affair of the state, the basis of life and death, the Way (Tao) to survival or extinction. It must be thoroughly pondered and analyzed.

Sun Tzu

Executive Summary

As security professionals we must accept the fact that conflict is a normal part of our professional and personal lives. Far from being an unnatural phenomenon that must be either avoided at all costs or waged with the goal of absolute destruction, conflict can be beneficial. Those who manage conflict well obtain efficient victories; those who fail to manage conflict well exhaust their resources and are eventually defeated.

How we and others view conflict is largely based on how we answer some fundamental questions about life and human nature.

1. What is the natural state of human beings?

2. Are people basically good or basically evil?

3. Is life about cooperation or competition?

Most business-related conflicts involve one or more of the following causes:

1. Differing objectives

2. Limited resources

3. Position and influence

4. Interpersonal matters

This chapter discusses each of the aforementioned causes of conflict and outlines three steps to understanding conflict.

1. Accept the inevitability of conflict.

2. Understand that conflict is not necessarily bad.

3. Make a systematic study of conflict typologies and decide how they apply to the operational environment.

Conflict Is Inevitable

The inevitability of conflict is made manifest in every field of human endeavor. Nations strive with nations. Workers strive with employers. Parents strive with children. Children strive with siblings. Sports teams exist for the very purpose of ritualized conflict, and the poor have struggled against the rich since the beginning of civilization. Both the electoral and judicial processes are adversarial in nature. One of the basic tenets of literature is the presence of conflict, be it human versus human, nature, self, or society. Even television and other forms of entertainment have taken the idea of conflict to new levels. We can now watch someone get voted off an island, dumped by Mr. or Ms. Right, or ridiculed by talent scouts, whenever we desire.

Is it then surprising that conflict should shape our day-to-day lives? Who has ever seriously dreamed of accomplishment without struggle or riches without work? Does any human being have unlimited resources? Is any organization completely secure? The reality is that conflict is inevitable. As security professionals, we can either accept that fact and prepare, or ignore reality and continually be defeated.

To begin to understand the nature of conflict, we must first answer some basic questions about life and the nature of human beings.

World-View and Conflict

What is the natural state of human beings? Are people basically good or basically evil? Is life about cooperation or competition? These questions reveal much about one's world-view and, by extension, the need to study conflict.

On one extreme are those who have not been exposed to significant security-related conflict. Based on their experience they are, not surprisingly, under the impression that conflict is unnecessary. This outlook makes them prone to ignore warning signs about possible danger and blame societal forces for "making" otherwise "good" people victimize others.

Does this sound familiar to you? As a security manager it's very likely that you've encountered people who hold this world-view. These are often the same people who deny the possibility that intentional malicious acts could be directed against your organization. Since the threats that you are warning them about fall outside their direct experience, it is difficult (but not impossible) to convince them.

At the other extreme are those for whom conflict has become a way of life. These people view the world as a zero-sum game in which winners win by denying others their legitimate needs. They create conflict where it can be avoided, and they expend resources in a never-ending series of pyrrhic battles.

As a security professional, this attitude may also sound familiar to you. Potentially violent employees, customers, or contractors often display remarkably similar views as those expressed above. These people will often blame others for their own shortcomings, have elevated frustration with the environment, exhibit paranoid behavior, and engage in socially unacceptable behavior toward others (Baron, 1993). Even if one never becomes violent, this extreme world-view and accompanying ideology surrounding conflict can cause disruptions of business and decreased morale.

The first world-view, if taken to its logical conclusion, results in an irresponsible lack of vigilance and victimization. The second world-view inevitably leads to anger, arrogance, and destruction. Thankfully, there is a middle ground.

As the opening quote of this chapter clearly indicates, Sun Tzu readily understood that conflict in the form of military action was essential to the survival and security of the state. In Sun Tzu's view, the nation that systematically studied and applied strategy would not only survive the challenges of hostile competitors, but would flourish. Conversely, the nation that failed to make a systematic study of military matters would find itself the captive of larger, more powerful enemies.

The strategically minded security professional is in much the same position. By constantly assessing threats to the organization and devising countermeasures that use as few resources as possible, the security professional can effectively counter legitimate threats without causing unnecessary conflicts and the accompanying drain of resources.

Business World Conflicts

Every security professional knows that the business world has no shortage of conflicts. Whether these conflicts are internal or external in nature, they can generally be divided into four categories: conflicts over objectives, conflicts over resources, conflicts over influence, and interpersonal conflicts.

Conflicts over Objectives

Conflicts originating out of differing or opposite objectives are very common. For a security professional, the most obvious example is manifested in his or her mandate to prevent organizational losses. Criminals who seek to steal, defraud, or damage organizational assets have exactly opposite objectives from those of the security manager. This type of conflict is unavoidable; much of the reason for having a Security Department is to prevent and/or mitigate losses.

Other objective-oriented conflicts can be more subtle. Take a bank branch, for example. In an effort to prevent robbers and irate customers from jumping the counter and assaulting employees, the bank's Security Department may want to install teller line barriers from floor to ceiling. Conversely, the bank's Safety Department may want to have lower barriers with open teller stations in order to reduce the number and severity of repetitive motion claims on the part of employees. Finally, the Marketing Department may want to eliminate barriers altogether in an effort to make the branch appear friendlier and more inviting to customers.

Depending on where one sits within the organization, any of these objectives can seem reasonable. It is therefore incumbent upon the security professional to learn as much about the objectives of other departments as possible. Doing so will enable creative solutions to be developed.

Conflicts over Resources

A classic business example of resource conflict is the annual budget process. Since businesses have limited resources, executive management has to decide how to allocate available funds in such a way as to make the firm most profitable. Budget allocations directly translate into new equipment, additions or deletions to staff, training, travel, and other critical department needs. As a result, resources conflicts are common. The strategically minded security manager will learn to quantitatively align his or her department's objectives and proposed resource allocation with those of the firm.

Conflicts over Influence

Conflicts arising out of a struggle for influence are also common in the business world. At a certain level within all organizations, there are managers who seek to have their vision for the firm translated into action. The extent to which one has the ability to have this vision implemented by those who hold power is a measure of influence. As a security professional, the development of influence with strategic policymakers is the key to success.

Interpersonal Conflicts

Interpersonal conflicts are most often based on lack of effective communication, pride, and emotionalism. As a result, they can provoke some of the most costly battles in business and should therefore be avoided if at all possible. When someone allows pride and raw emotionalism to control their actions, they are likely to make decisions that, under normal circumstances, they would never consider. Interpersonal conflicts may result in loud, disruptive arguments, acts of covert sabotage, and even acts of violence.

The Security Manager and Conflict

Security professionals generally understand that conflict with criminals and other traditional threat vectors is part and parcel of the field. What many professionals fail to see is the fact that conflict isn't always overt and doesn't always involve traditional security issues. Most often, security professionals will find themselves in conflict with other departments over influence, resources, or objectives. At other times, the conflict may be trying to convince senior management that the best course of action is the one being recommended by the security manager. At yet other times, the conflict may be interpersonal and involve smoothing over relationships.

In order to successfully manage conflict at all levels, the security professional needs to:

1. Accept the inevitability of conflict.

2. Understand that conflict is not necessarily bad.

3. Make a systematic study of conflict typologies and decide how they apply to the operational environment.

Chapter 3 Scenario

The Corporate Security Department of a biotechnology firm in the Southeast was composed of several groups, including Security Operations, Investigations, and Information Security. These groups were all professionally run by highly qualified experts in their respective disciplines. Unfortunately, they all shared a common problem. Each of these groups had an ongoing rivalry with at least one of the other groups.

- The Investigations Group thought that those in Operations were inexperienced and, therefore, not as professional as their own personnel. As a result, they distrusted the Operations Group. This showed when the groups had to work together.

- The Operations Group looked upon the Investigations personnel as being aloof, arrogant, and uncooperative. As a result, they looked for opportunities to show up the Investigations Group.

- The Information Security Group had very little dealings with the Operations Group and distrusted the Investigations Group. As a result, Information Security was slow to provide the requisite data needed to pursue cases.

On the rare occurrences when employees transferred from one group to another, they soon found themselves not accepted by their new group and treated as traitors by their old group. As time passed, these rivalries resulted in critical mistakes that reflected on the entire Corporate Security Department. Eventually, the department was reorganized, and several positions were eliminated.

1. How would you characterize these conflicts? Are they conflict of objectives, conflict of resources, conflict of influence, or interpersonal conflicts? Why?

2. If you were the chief security officer of this organization, what steps would you take to overcome the situation described above?

3. If you were an employee who just transferred from one department to another, how would you become accepted by your new colleagues, while still maintaining a good relationship with your former colleagues?

Discussion Questions

1. Why is it important to study conflict?

2. Do you believe that conflict is inevitable? Why or why not?

3. Based on the type of conflicts discussed in Chapter 2, which do you find to be the most difficult to deal with and why?

4. Describe an area of conflict at your organization and how it might be best handled.

4 *Know Yourself and Know Your Enemy*

> *If you know others and know yourself, you will not be imperiled in a hundred battles.*
>
> Sun Tzu

Executive Summary

Sun Tzu aptly noted that generals who knew both themselves and their adversaries would not be imperiled in one hundred battles, but that those who knew only themselves or knew only their enemies would prevail only half of the time. Still worse, Sun Tzu predicted that those leaders who knew neither themselves nor their opponents would be in peril during every conflict.

Today's security professional faces a similar situation. On one hand, the security manager is charged with the familiar territory of protecting the organization from external criminal elements. Most security managers are comfortable with this role and spend a great deal of time examining external threats to their organization. While many tend to focus on finding vulnerabilities with the firm as a whole, few apply this lesson to their specific department or to internal competitors.

This chapter provides a general overview of both external and internal adversaries commonly faced by today's security professional. A checklist is provided at the end of the book (Appendix: The Armory) to help security managers better know themselves and their adversary, whether the adversary is a criminal gang or a legitimate internal group competing for the same budget resources.

Who Is the Enemy?

One cannot hope to direct an army, business, or security organization without a complete understanding and identification of one's adversaries. The array of adversaries that stands between a security manager and his or her objectives can be quite diverse. Foreknowledge of an adversary's intentions and capabilities will enable the security manager to adapt to an ever-changing "battlefield." The security manager's adversaries may be generally divided into two broad groups: external adversaries and internal adversaries.

External Adversaries

External adversaries consist of hostile actors not employed by the target organization. External adversaries fall into the following four categories:

Criminals

Competitors

Terrorists

Activists

Criminals

Criminal activity is found in all organizations and at all levels of society. The successful security manager will learn to recognize the risk and vulnerability of his or her organization to the various forms of criminal activity and implement business-friendly countermeasures to prevent or mitigate impacts.

- **Petty criminals**

Petty criminals are probably the most common adversary faced by a security manager. Individual incidents caused by these adversaries will generally result in relatively small financial losses to the organization. There are, however, exceptions, including the theft of a laptop or jump-drive that happens to contain confidential company and/or consumer information. Additional problems can include a deterioration of morale on the part of employees as caused by

1. Small, but frequently occurring financial losses

2. Vandalism to property

When dealing with petty criminal activity, the security manager must constantly balance risk against the expense of the countermeasures and potential losses. While this is true of all security-related matters, it is particularly pronounced with petty crimes such as vandalism, where the incidents are less costly but more frequent.

- **Violent criminals**

Any type of criminal incident that can occur in society can occur in the workplace. Violent crime is a significant problem for all security managers. The occurrence of an assault, robbery, rape, or homicide can have devastating effects on the enterprise, including:

1. Loss of personnel involved

2. Increased turnover and decreased productivity

3. Low morale, fear, and distrust

4. Civil liability and related legal expenses

5. Increases in security, safety, and insurance expenditures

6. Counseling expenses

7. Damage to public reputation

8. Possible reduction in customer traffic

Given the aforementioned potential impacts of a violent crime in the workplace, security professionals must be cognizant of the risks and vulnerabilities associated with these adversaries.

- **Professional criminals**

While most people choose legitimate work as tradesmen, pubic servants, or business professionals, there are a subset of individuals who choose to ignore moral and ethical conventions to become professional criminals. Some specialize in burglary, some in robbery, and others in fraud. Just as every legitimate field has innumerable niches in which to specialize, so, too, does the illegitimate career of a professional criminal. While professional criminals who specialize in a given "discipline" are less common than either petty or violent criminals, they can still pose significant difficulties for the security professional. Some of these difficulties include:

1. **Organization:** The professional conducts research, striking at known vulnerabilities.

2. **Timing:** The professional strikes when the opportunity for success is high.

3. **Specialization:** The professional has specific niche expertise.

When dealing with the professional criminal, the security manager should make use of high-quality intelligence obtained from colleagues, professional organizations, academic research, and liaison with public authorities. Administratively, the security manager should be conducting continual risk and vulnerability assessments of the facilities and organization. Operationally, the security manager should ensure that an element of unpredictability is added to the routines of the security department.

- **Organized criminal enterprises**

Organized crime is professional and well funded, and possesses an international reach. Organized criminal organizations are involved in drugs, prostitution, weapons smuggling, fraud, pornography, piracy, and a host of other vices that destabilize society. Problems associated with organized criminal enterprises can include:

1. **Organization:** Organized criminal enterprises are highly organized, with a somewhat cellular structure similar to that of a terrorist organization. As a result, it is difficult to dismantle the organization.

2. **Resources:** Organized criminal enterprises generally have greater resources available to commit to battle and are not constrained by regulations, laws, morality, or ethics.

3. **Covert:** It is common for organized criminal enterprises to infiltrate target organizations through planting an operative as an employee or intimidating current employees to serve as conduits of information.

The security manager who deals with an organized criminal enterprise cannot hope to win on his or her own. Law enforcement and other allied organizations must be involved.

Competitors

Competition is the cornerstone of the free enterprise system. It is through competition that ideas are implemented into action and the global standard of living is raised over time. In today's information-based economy, a significant element of competition is the effective utilization of business intelligence. When discussing business intelligence, it is important to note that the collection and analysis of business information need not be illegal or unethical. In most instances, open-source information such as published newspaper and magazine articles, Web sites, and public documents are a legal means by which information can be obtained.

Unfortunately, there will always be competitors who are willing to go beyond legitimate business intelligence into the world of corporate espionage. While the public typically thinks of espionage as either something that occurs only in movies or as an activity conducted exclusively by governments, the security professional cannot afford such naivete. Security managers must be prepared to deal with the very real possibility of corporate espionage whether it comes from domestic or foreign firms.

- **Business intelligence and corporate espionage methods**

A host of methods are available, both legal and illegal, by which an adversary can gain vital business information about your firm. These methods include:

1. **Open source information**
   Open-source information is legal and may include newspapers, magazines, trade journals, Web sites, academic research, publicly available government reports, and documents, as well as networking through professional organizations or social contacts.

2. **Use of investigators**
   Most often companies legally utilize investigators to gather specific business-related information; however, this is not always the case. There are some disreputable investigators who will gather information without regard for the law and with no questions asked.

3. **Dumpster diving**
   This method doesn't always involve illegal activity. In fact, it doesn't even always involve dumpsters. In some jurisdictions, an investigator can legally take trash that is put out on a curb for pick-up. This is important for a security manager as draft memos, reports, spreadsheets, data storage devices, and other potentially damaging items are often thrown away.

4. **Unauthorized undercover operatives**
   Many firms hire private investigators to work covertly inside their faculties and report back on criminal activity or violations of company policy. These issues may include theft, drug use, and sexual harassment, to name a few. Unfortunately, the same methods used by the firm to spot illegal and unethical activities can be used against it by a competitor. The security manager needs to be cognizant of the background investigation process and unusual activities among employees. In addition, the security manager needs to work with other departments and senior management to ensure that logical and physical access is restricted to the information an employee needs to do his or her job. Finally, the security manager needs to ensure that employees are educated on how to spot and report unusual activity.

5. **Listening devices, storage devices, and cameras**
   Advances in electronic and wireless technology, combined with a trend toward increased user-friendliness, have resulted in inexpensive and easily concealable tools for espionage. The presence of a listening device

or a camera inside a board room or executive office could result in the compromise of marketing strategy, product development plans, and a host of other confidential information. The deployment of such devices can be easily carried out by compromised or disgruntled employees as well as people posing as service personnel. Add to this scenario the presence of cellular telephones with built-in, Internet-accessible cameras and video recorders, as well as portable disk drives, including MP3 players, and it becomes easy to realize how vulnerable most businesses are to corporate espionage.

The security manager needs to constantly educate himself or herself, as well as senior management and employees, about the threat. In addition, the successful security manager will work with other departments to establish policies and procedures necessary to mitigate the threat.

6. **Social engineering**

Social engineering is a psychosocial technique designed to obtain confidential information through misrepresentation, misdirection, and manipulation of a target. Those engaged in social engineering techniques often do so via telephone or e-mail; however, the technique can be used in face-to-face encounters as well.

A social engineer will engage in misrepresentation by contacting the target and pretending to be someone who has legitimate access to the data being sought. Even without passwords or other authenticators, this technique is often successful. Alternatively, the social engineer may misdirect the target by pretending to be working for someone who should have direct access to the information. The social engineer who encounters a target that doubts the pretext may attempt to manipulate the target by being overly friendly, engaging in flirtation, or being intimidating. The social engineer may also try to play on the target's sense of duty, compassion, guilt, or any other perceived weakness.

One common version of a social engineering attempt is an e-mail solicitation received from abroad. Because many of these letters originate in Nigeria, they have come to be known as "419 Letters," named for the section of the Nigerian penal code that deals with fraud. These letters claim to be from someone in authority. Sometimes this person is a foreign general or government official. At other times the writer claims to be a company president, banker, or even a member of the clergy member. After a long-winded and often poorly written cover story, the writer solicits the recipient's assistance in moving a large sum of money to the United States with a promise of a fee.

Continual education efforts and assessment through social penetration testing by the security department can go a long way toward countering this threat. However, human nature being what it is, this technique will always be an effective weapon that the security manager needs to guard against.

7. **Hacking**

The ongoing trend toward an enterprise risk management model with its accompanying convergence of protective functions, under one umbrella, necessitates that the security manager have an understanding of network security. As with all other types of security, the protection of the corporate network requires an interdisciplinary approach, based on risks, vulnerabilities, and the potential impacts of identified threats. The successful security manager will educate himself or herself on other areas of security and will endeavor to form working partnerships with other departments including information technology, business continuity, and disaster recovery.

8. **Compromise of employees**

It is often said that employees are an organization's most valuable asset. Not coincidentally, they are also the most easily compromised by adversaries. This compromise generally happens in one of two ways—extortion or bribery.

Employees can be subjected to extortion by threats of physical violence against either themselves or their families. This is the approach often utilized by organized criminal enterprises such as gangs. Another way that employees can be extorted is by threats to reveal information that, if made public, would damage the individual. These situations can be either discovered and subsequently used by an adversary or even engineered. Does the employee have a gambling habit? Has he done something illegal that he thinks no one knows about? Is he involved or prone to be involved in an extramarital affair? Does he use drugs? Does he use alcohol to excess? Under the right circumstances an adversary can use any of these factors to compromise an employee's loyalty and thereby elicit confidential information.

Employees can also be compromised through bribery. Is the employee dissatisfied with her compensation? Is she in debt? Does she want another position? An adversary can offer jobs, money, and other perks that can result in compromise as well.

The successful security manager will keep a close eye on factors that can lead to compromise and, where possible, work with senior management, human resources, and business line managers to ensure that employees are not compromised by external adversaries.

Government-Supported Economic Espionage: A Case Study

On July 8, 1990, Mark Goldberg was arrested in Palo Alto, California, and charged with theft of trade secrets from his then employer, Renaissance Software. Further investigation revealed that Mr. Goldberg, a French citizen, had come to the United States in the late 1980s under a French government-sponsored program that allowed young men an alternative to compulsory military service.

The program provided government compensation to the participants, who, in return would write reports about their work experience in the United States. Originally, Goldberg worked at Connecticut-based MUST Software, but later moved to Palo Alto where he worked at Renaissance, a firm that specialized in the creation of software for financial services companies.

As Goldberg's program was coming to an end and he gave his notice to his employers at Renaissance, his work habits began to change. He began visiting the office at hours that were unusual for him. This behavior tipped off company officials, who after investigating his access to computer logs discovered that he had downloaded confidential information on several projects, including those that had nothing to do with his position at Renaissance.

After company officials confronted Goldberg about the information, he admitted to taking the files and gave the officials some tapes that he claimed had the information on them. A subsequent review of the tapes indicated that the tapes were blank. Goldberg was arrested at the airport the next day as he was about to catch a flight to France. Despite diplomatic pressure from the French government, Goldberg was subsequently convicted, given a suspended sentence, and ordered to community service. He later returned to France.

This case and others like it illustrate how many foreign governments, not just France, target proprietary business information. As Pierre Marion, former director of France's Direction Generale de la Securité Exterieure (DSGE) put it, "This espionage activity is an essential way for France to keep abreast of international commerce and technology. Of course, it was directed against the United States as well as others. You must remember that while we are allies in defense matters, we are also economic competitors in the world."

Today's security professional must be aware of the threat not only of company-on-company espionage but of government-sponsored intelligence as well (Nolan, 2000, Phoenix Consulting Group).

Terrorists

Terrorism is a form of asymmetrical warfare, utilized by nongovernmental actors to further their agendas through acts of violence or coercion directed against the populace.

Unlike traditional warfare, combatants do not meet on a battlefield and are not part of a recognized military force. Instead, terrorist organizations seek to cause fear among the populace by creating uncertainty. This uncertainty eventually undermines the target population's trust in the government, thus creating instability and, if left unchecked, eventually leading to a change in government or policies (MIPT Terrorist Knowledge Base).

Terrorist Group Typologies

Terrorist organizations generally fall into one of three categories: ideological/political, religious, or single issue. The objective of the ideological/political terrorist organization is to establish a government structure that is in line with the political philosophies or separatist ideologies of the group. Examples of ideological/political terrorist organizations include left-wing organizations such as Action Direct, the Red Brigades, the Japanese Red Army, and the Tupac Amaru Revolutionary Movement, to name a few. Examples of right-wing terrorist organizations include the Arizona Patriots, United Self Defense Forces of Venezuela, Fatherland and Liberty National Front, and the Anti-communist Command (MIPT Terrorist Knowledge Base).

The objective of religious-based terrorist organizations is to fulfill the members' faith through violent means. Religious-based terrorist organizations are typically offshoots of mainstream religious beliefs that have come to believe that violence is the only way to accomplish what they see as their God's will on earth. Because of their zeal, religious-based terrorist organizations can be some of the most difficult to combat. Examples of religious-based terrorist organizations include Al Qaeda, Aum Shiri Kyo, Divine Wrath Brigades, and Hezbollah (MIPT Terrorist Knowledge Base).

As the name of the third category suggests, the objective of the single-issue based terrorist organization is very specific. These single issues may be social, political, environmental, economic, or any one of a myriad of other causes. Examples of single-issue terrorist organizations include Earth First, the Animal Liberation Front, Earth Liberation Front, and Revolutionary Cells Animal Liberation Brigade (MIPT Terrorist Knowledge Base).

Terrorist Strategy

Terrorism is asymmetrical in that it involves the use of unorthodox techniques against undefended or lightly defended civilian targets. In other words, the operational cost of a terrorist act is minor when compared to the damage inflicted on the enemy and the subsequent influence generated for the group. Recent examples of terrorism illustrate this return on investment (MIPT Terrorist Knowledge Base).

The attacks of September 11, 2001, involved 19 identified hijackers and most likely several dozen additional and unidentified support personnel. Through this investment, al Qaeda toppled the Twin Towers, damaged the Pentagon, and killed over three thousand people. Beyond the direct operational effects resulting from the attacks, al Qaeda made further gains as well. The stock market fell precipitously, civil aviation temporarily ground to a halt, and the government of the United States conducted one of the largest departmental reorganizations in history (Haddow and Bullock; 9/11 Commission Report). Most importantly, al Qaeda became known, and in some places respected, throughout the world, thus generating a platform from which to advance its agenda.

The subsequent anthrax attacks and numerous "white powder" incidents provide yet another example of the effectiveness of this type of asymmetrical warfare. A small number of actual anthrax attacks created hysteria and tied up federal, state, and local law enforcement resources, as well as corporate security and fire personnel, for months.

The Madrid railway attacks of March 11, 2004, also produced a significant return on investment for terrorists. By placing several bombs on commuter trains, the terrorists were able to influence the Spanish elections, effectively removing Spain from the U.S.-led coalition fighting in Iraq.

By engaging in seemingly random acts of violence, the terrorist organization can disrupt day-to-day life to such an extent that its cause is eventually placed on the nation's political agenda.

Government Responses

Targeted governments have traditionally responded to terrorist organizations by either capitulating to their demands or seeking to combat the terrorists through the use of police, security, intelligence, and military assets. When governments have capitulated, it has typically occurred after a long period of unsuccessful attempts to arrest or destroy the terrorist organization. The longer a government remains unsuccessful at stopping terrorist actions, the more credibility it loses. This process is exacerbated when attempts to crack down on terrorism result in prolonged encroachments on civil liberties and abuse of power by frustrated government forces.

Targeted governments that do not capitulate to terrorist demands typically go through a long period of low-intensity conflict, involving a necessary increase in defensive and emergency response posture. This often also results in a temporary reduction of civil liberties and internal criticism of government policies. Over time, the successful government will "win the hearts and minds" of the populace first, thus undermining the terrorist organization's ability to hide. Once this is accomplished, it will lead to solid intelligence that can be exploited by police and military forces.

Terrorist Tactics

The range of tactics employed by the terrorist organization is limited only by the resources and ingenuity of the leadership. Common tactics utilized by terrorist organizations include, but are not limited to, kidnapping, assassination, armed assault, bombing, hijacking, and sabotage.

The success of a terrorist operation is dependent on preoperational intelligence, internal security, and commitment by the members of the organization. Preoperational intelligence may include detailed surveillance of the target for weeks, months, or even years at a time. It may also include the collection of both open-source and privately held data. Terrorist operatives may attempt to infiltrate the target organization by securing employment, posing as employees, or employing time-tested social engineering techniques.

The internal security employed by a terrorist organization is based on the same principles utilized by government, military, and corporate security professionals. Namely, the terrorist leadership recruits operatives over long periods of time, conducts background research, and gradually increases the recruit's responsibilities over time. In addition, the terrorist organization is compartmentalized into a cellular structure in which one member of one cell may know only one member of another cell. This structure prevents the entire organization from being compromised should one member or a small group be arrested. In many cases, this structure is further divided by responsibilities in which one cell may be responsible for preoperational surveillance, another for obtaining supplies, another for securing financing, and still another for carrying out the attack.

The commitment of the terrorist organization's members is dependent on a wide variety of factors, including the cause itself, the leadership, and the actions of their adversaries.

The Security Professional and Terrorism

Terrorism represents a significant threat to the economic well-being of any organization. Even firms that are unlikely to be a direct target of a terrorist operation need to plan for collateral damage in the form of employee deaths, loss of vital information, damaged property, and sustained business interruption. In order to even begin to successfully mitigate the threat of terrorism, the security professional needs to employ a multidisciplinary, all-hazards strategy. An understanding of terrorist organizations, risk and vulnerability assessment, physical security, crisis management, and the intelligence process are essential to securing a facility against terrorism.

When reviewing the security posture of a facility, the following are some basic questions that should be addressed:

1. Does senior management support the security program?
2. How does security fit in with the overall mission of the organization?
3. What are the specific risks and vulnerabilities of the particular operating environment?
4. What is the most effective means of allocating the organization's risk management budget?
5. What crisis management plans are in place?
6. Are the crisis management plans adequate?
7. How would management ensure the safety of employees?
8. Have the organization's emergency plans been exercised?
9. Do employees fully understand their roles?
10. Do the current emergency plans take into account organizational security and business continuity issues?

Proactive Observation and Awareness: The Keys to Success

The following steps are taken from an awareness poster released by the New York State Metropolitan Transit Authority. This poster contained some common recommendations for recognizing a burgeoning terrorist operation before it reaches the attack stage:

1. **Counter-surveillance:** Security personnel and employees need to be watchful for people conducting surveillance of the facility. Surveillance may include photographs, video, notes, drawings, or simply observation.

2. **Social engineering and information gathering:** Security personnel and employees need to be wary of people trying to directly or indirectly solicit information on or demonstrating an unusual interest in building systems, security procedures, schedules, organizational structures, or similar information.

3. **Probing:** Security personnel and employees need to be wary of people attempting to test security measures of a given facility or organization. Hostile actors may attempt to gain surreptitious entry to a facility, leave unidentified parcels in common areas to observe the response of security, or otherwise find ways to compromise the integrity of the security program.

4. **Obtaining equipment:** Merchants, security personnel, and employees should be aware of attempts to obtain explosives, weapons, or other material that may be utilized to carry out a terrorist incident.

5. **Awareness:** The organization that focuses on security personnel and employee awareness will more likely than not "fail" a terrorist organization's target selection criteria. Although these steps may not prevent a terrorist attack from occurring, they may deflect or delay the attack to another facility, or increase the chance of intervention by law enforcement agencies.

Terrorist incidents don't happen every day, but emergencies can and do happen anywhere, anytime, and anyplace. The successful security program will address all the aforementioned areas by implementing an all-hazards approach. Only by doing so can an organization hope to be prepared to deal with the threat of terrorism (NYS Metropolitan Transit Authority).

Activists

A focus on political freedom and democratic principles accounts for much of the strength of Western society. Ensuring that citizens have the right to worship, assemble, petition, speak, write, and even protest against the government or other organizations creates a sanctioned method for societal change. The presence of these sanctioned methods actually results in a safety valve of sorts. Individuals and organizations that may, under different circumstances, resort to violence, are given a peaceful alternative.

Given this framework, the vast majority of protesters do not represent a significant physical threat to an organization's security. Some groups, however, have come to the conclusion that sanctioned methods of social change won't work, and so they have therefore resorted to criminal activity and violence.

Many of these organizations have either single issues or very small platforms that are a focus of their activities. While no one side has a monopoly with regard to overstepping the bounds of law, the following topics are often the driving force behind the controversies:

1. Abortion

2. Animal rights

3. Anti-taxes

4. Environmental interests

5. Eschatology and doomsday cults

6. Fair trade/free trade

7. Gun rights

8. Ideology and religious beliefs

9. Organized labor and management

10. Race relations and separatist groups

Activist Techniques

Social activists rely heavily on public exposure to attract followers and funding as well as to get their message out and on society's agenda. Activists may utilize legal means, illegal means, or a hybrid of the two to achieve their objectives. Some of these methods may include:

1. Court challenges and injunctions

2. Sit-ins or chaining of oneself to a business

3. Vandalism or sabotage

4. Arson or bomb threats

5. Violence

6. Large public rallies

7. Public relations offensives and petitions

When dealing with activist groups, the security professional must rely heavily on information-gathering techniques and on a solid knowledge of the types of assets most likely to be targeted.

Internal Adversaries

In addition to the external adversaries we've just discussed, the security professional must also be prepared to deal with internal adversaries. Internal adversaries may be grouped into two general categories:

1. Personnel issues—employee or contractor

2. Other departments

Personnel Issues

Unethical employees and contractors pose a significant threat to the security of the organization. The fact that these people have authorized access to the facility, understand policies and procedures, and blend into the day-to-day landscape of normal business operations gives them ample opportunity for misappropriating a whole host of assets. The greater the level of responsibility given to the employee or contractor, the greater their ability to cause damage. Some common personnel issues include:

1. Lax attitudes
   a. "It can't happen here"
   b. Security is an "inconvenience"
   c. Perfunctory compliance with policies
   d. Awareness without concern
2. Employee theft or unauthorized use of
   a. Equipment
   b. Money
   c. Time
   d. Information
   e. Personal enrichment
3. Harassment
   a. Sexual
   b. Race based
4. Internal crime
   a. Insider trading
   b. Fraud
   c. Drugs
   d. Workplace violence

Other departments within the organization may also manifest themselves as internal adversaries. As outlined in Chapter 3, issues with other departments are typically caused by struggles over objectives, resources, influence, or interpersonal conflict. The security manager must be cognizant of potential conflicts with other departments and attempt to avoid or diffuse them whenever possible; only engaging is direct battle where absolutely necessary. Although every organization is different, some common internal adversaries that come from other departments can include:

1. **Safety:** Although counterintuitive, Safety and Security departments often have conflicts over objectives. While both want employees to be safe and secure, the priorities given to specific controls or countermeasures often put these two departments at odds.

2. **Human resources:** Conflicts between Security and the Human Resources departments are often the result of misunderstandings. Some Security professionals look upon Human Resources professionals as being too concerned about individual employee rights at the expense of the firm as a whole. Some Human Resources professionals see Security professionals as being too distrustful of employees; ready to investigate or suggest termination instead of solving problems in other ways. The reality is that both departments are essential and must work together. Frequent meetings and short-term internships can go a long way toward solving these issues.

3. **Facilities:** The natural inclination of Facilities personnel is to hold down costs. As a result, they often look upon Security as being too ready to suggest expensive equipment and other countermeasures. Conversely, Security often looks at Facilities as being unconcerned about employee safety.

4. **Marketing:** Marketing personnel have a vested interest in making customers feel welcomed. This is understandable and necessary for the continued functioning of an enterprise. Security personnel have a vested interest in controlling the environment in an effort to prevent crime and other loss events. As with the previous examples, finding a happy medium and developing strong relationships is the key to success.

Internal Competitors

Beyond dealing with the traditional threats to security posed by criminals, terrorists, unethical employees, and their ilk, today's security manager must also compete for his department's share of influence and resources. Depending on the specific organizational structure in place, internal competitors could arise from any quarter of the firm. Most commonly, security departments often find themselves in conflict with other service departments, but business lines may be competitors as well.

When dealing with internal competitors, the security manager must seek to understand the adversary's position as well as his or her organization's own position.

Discussion Questions

1. Who are your most dangerous external adversaries and why?

2. Who are your most significant internal competitors?

3. How do your most significant internal competitors stack up against your department?

4. Do you think a competitor in one area can be an ally in another area? Why or why not?

5. How does Sun Tzu's concept of knowing oneself and one's enemy apply to your situation?

6. What measures can you use to determine how much influence you have in your organization?

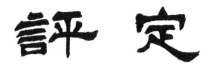

5 *Conduct Strategic Assessments*

The one who figures on victory at headquarters before even doing battle is the one with the most strategic factors on his side. The one who figures on inability to prevail at headquarters before doing battle is the one who has the least strategic factors on his side. The one with many strategic factors in his favor wins, the one with few strategic factors in his favor loses—how much more so for the one with no strategic factors in his favor. Observing this matter in this way, I can see who will win and who will lose.

Sun Tzu

Executive Summary

The cornerstone of every security program is the accurate and dispassionate assessment of the organizational purpose, associated risks, vulnerabilities, and potential impacts to the assets being protected. Sun Tzu's *The Art of War* recognized this some 2500 years ago when discussing how to assess whether or not one could prevail in battle.

Sun Tzu recommended that generals assess the conditions to determine:

1. Who possesses the greater moral authority or "The Way"?
2. Which side can better take advantage of the "weather" or external influence?
3. Which side can take better advantage of the "terrain" or operational environment?
4. Which side has better leaders or managers?
5. Which side has a better system of reward and discipline?

This chapter applies those strategic assessment questions to today's business and security environment.

In Chapter 3, we discussed the inevitability of conflict in all areas of human endeavor. Once we have accepted this inevitability, we must then make plans to deal with the multitude of conflicts that we are likely to face. A systematic approach to the study of conflict is necessary if we are to be serious in our intentions. This systematic study must start by the conduct of strategic assessment of one's self and one's adversary, and the conditions in which the two forces will meet.

Strategy and Tactics

When discussing the terms *strategy* and *tactics*, people often use them interchangeably. In colloquial conversation, the lack of distinction isn't noticeable. When speaking professionally, however, it is important to understand that the two words differ in terms of scope and complexity.

Strategy refers to an overarching and often complex plan to achieve a goal. A strategy may employ various resources and methods, called tactics, to achieve a series of smaller, more clearly defined objectives. These smaller objectives, in turn, support the aforementioned departmental goals. Departmental goals then support organizational goals, which, in turn, support the business needs of the organization.

Figure 5-1   *Strategy requires an alignment of resources, tactics, and objectives.*

Conversely, **tactics** refers to the specific methodological details needed to achieve individual objectives that, when completed, support the overall strategy of the department and organization. Tactics may involve the use of equipment, patrol strategies, staffing schemes, and a host of other conventional and unconventional means.

To put it in terms of warfare, a general assigned to direct the overall military conduct of the war or theater of operations would be said to be engaged in strategic-level leadership. Officers assigned to lead troops in individual battles or engagements would be said to be involved in tactical leadership. In the security world, a strategic manager may direct the organization's overall security needs. A tactical leader may lead a group of security officers, investigators, etcetera, in the pursuit of day-to-day activities.

Sun Tzu's View of Strategic Assessments

In *The Art of War*, Sun Tzu provided five criteria for assessing the capabilities of an adversary (Cleary).

- **The Way:** Which political leadership has the ability to maintain the loyal following of the populace? As Sun Tzu noted, leaders who cultivate "The Way" induce the people to have the same aim as the leadership so that they would "share death and share life without fear of danger."

- **Weather:** What are the conditions of the times, and whom do they favor? Is it raining or snowing? If so, how does this affect the movement of the army?

- **Terrain:** What are the conditions of the battlefield and the approaches thereof? Can the army utilize the terrain to its advantage? Do high bluffs provide a vantage point from which to observe the movement of the adversary? Do the field of battle and the approaches provide concealment or a means of escape?

- **Leadership:** Which general or battlefield leader has the greater ability? Which leader is more experienced? Which army's officers and NCOs are better trained? Do the troops respect their leaders?

- **Discipline:** Which side's systems of reward and punishment are clearer? Is the chain of command followed? Are officers arbitrary in their treatment of the soldiers? Who is more motivated?

Sun Tzu notes: "Every General has heard of these five things, those who know them prevail. Those who do not know them do not prevail" (translation by Cleary) (p. 5).

Sun Tzu's Strategic Assessments for the Security Manager

As security management professionals, we, too, must make assessments. These assessments most often include applicable risks, vulnerabilities, and the potential impacts of specified threats to a given facility or process. Less common, at least in the private sector, are strategic capability assessments of a specific adversary. We can apply Sun Tzu's five assessment criteria to the world of the security professional by using the following guidelines:

The Way: The Way indicates the overall character, sense of mission, or urgency with which an organization inculcates its employees. When senior management provides the employees with a sense of grand organizational objectives, employees are more likely to feel they are part of something bigger than themselves and thus will go the extra mile to accomplish the mission with a sense of urgency.

When assessing whether the leadership of an organization, department, or group properly cultivates "The Way," it is important to examine the organization's culture according to the following five factors:

1. Fundamental mission

2. Articulation and demonstration of the fundamental mission

3. People

4. Reputation

5. Organizational myths

Some questions that should be asked include the following.

- **Is there a sense of mission, or is it just a job?**

Given human nature and today's business environment, a sense of organizational mission beyond the profit motive is vital to the cultivation of "The Way."

Fundamentally, people work to support their material needs, but the specific choice of work is motivated by more than monetary benefits. While some may argue that those who choose low-paying jobs do so because they lack options, the evidence seems to suggest otherwise. People who work in the ministry typically have at least a master's-level education. Those who choose to work as a teacher must have at least a bachelor's degree and often possess advanced degrees as well. To be an emergency medical technician, firefighter, police officer, or public safety dispatcher doesn't require a great deal of formal education, but the amount of training and continuing education rivals or exceeds that of the more academically educated. Certainly, stay-at-home mothers, line-level security officers, and childcare workers are less motivated by money than by mission.

Even for those with highly sought-after skill sets, it is doubtful that material compensation is the sole or even prime motivator. Technology and the changing norms of the business world have created virtually limitless opportunities for those with the right skill sets. Competition among employers has led to flex-time, telecommuting, job-sharing, sabbaticals, and a host of other benefits that, years ago, would have been thought fanciful.

To cultivate "The Way," management needs to ensure that the organization exists not only to make a profit, but to provide a sense of mission.

- **Does the senior management of the organization articulate the organization's mission?**

A deep sense of mission cannot be created without the full support of senior management. Since managers set the tone for everything that happens in an organization, they must clearly articulate and demonstrate the organizational mission to the employees. Slogans are not enough, as employees are always watching to see that words and actions are in sync. Take, for example, two large firms based in the northeastern United States.

At one firm, management communications were consistently full of exhortations to provide a safe environment for employees and customers. However, when the firm's own safety and security personnel pointed out significant physical and procedural deficiencies at one of the firm's sites, they were pressured to destroy their findings and downplay the issues. These actions by individual members of senior management sent a loud, clear, and chilling message to the employees involved.

At another firm across town, management communications were similarly phrased, but here the words were combined with action. This was illustrated when a temporary employee was assigned to fill in for the receptionist on the executive floor. The temporary employee had never met the CEO and because of an oversight was not shown his photograph. When the CEO arrived, the temporary employee politely challenged him and confirmed his identity. The CEO was so impressed that a temporary employee had shown such diligence and responsibility that he found a full-time position for her. Once again, a message was clearly sent, but in this case, it encouraged employees to be more cognizant of security and safety.

- **What type of people work for the organization?**

The type of people employed by an organization speaks volumes about how the leadership cultivates "The Way." What do people who currently work for the organization say about it? Do employees seem committed, or are they biding their time until the next opportunity presents itself? What is the rate of turnover? Are employees compensated within industry norms? Are ethical processes valued, or are they sacrificed in the name of short-term results? Are employees continuing to learn and grow, or are they complacent?

What about former employees? Do people who have left the organization have positive things to say about it, or do they carry resentment and regret? While individuals can have significantly different experiences at the same firm, the results of multiple individuals taken in aggregate can inform the assessor. By observing a firm's employees, management, and advisers, one can ascertain the values of the organization.

- **What is the public reputation of the organization?**

Understanding an organization's reputation is essential in determining the extent to which management cultivates "The Way." While reputations are sometimes undeserved, the vast majority of the time there is at least a kernel of truth present. When assessing the reputation of an organization, ask yourself these questions: What type of media coverage has the organization and its principals received over a long period of time? How often has the organization been sued? How many regulatory fines has the organization received? What are the tone and content of the organization's public statements? By examining the organization's reputation, the assessor will be better informed and able to ascertain the overall "way" of the firm.

- **What corporate myths exist about the organization?**

Every organization has myths. These myths or corporate legends serve to illustrate the core belief of the organization. When assessing the overall "way" of the organization, it is important to examine these myths. Is there a common theme or set of themes present? If so, what do they say about the organization's culture? Are the themes of these corporate legends aligned with the mission statements and actions of management? By examining these organizational legends or myths, one can ascertain what an organization values.

Weather: In the context of Sun Tzu's *Art of War*, weather literally meant weather or seasons. In our context as security professionals, the term *weather* refers to external conditions that influence the behavior of our own group and/or that of our adversaries. It is important to remember that often these conditions, by themselves, affect both sides in a conflict equally. When assessing "weather" conditions, the security professional's observations are based on the context of the particular situation. Some external factors that could impact the mission may include:

1. Market conditions

2. Regulatory climate

3. Public relations issues

4. External political, religious, and other controversial issues

- **Market conditions**

Changes in market conditions affect the ability of management personnel to accomplish their missions. In times of surplus, organizations are more likely to fund aspects of security programs that, in times of instability, would be out of the question. In most instances, the market conditions will be the same for each side; this is not always the case, however. The ability of each side to deal with the existing conditions can differ considerably.

When assessing how market conditions affect each side, the security professional should ask the following questions:

1. Are market conditions equally distributed across the industry or firm? In other words, is the field of play equally difficult for both sides?

2. What resources does each side possess?

3. Is each side able to utilize its given resources equally?

4. Which side has the most successful experience in dealing with similar market conditions?

By asking these questions and others like them, security professionals should be able to ascertain whether or not the market conditions that affect their operations are equal or unequal to that of their adversary.

- **Regulatory climate**

While government regulations have a significant impact on the operation of all business units, these impacts are more pronounced for the disciplines related to risk management–disciplines of security, safety, and business continuity. The reason for this is that most government mandates are directly related to the protection of workers, the environment, critical infrastructure, or information.

Since a significant expenditure of funds, as well as enhanced reporting and record keeping, is often a prerequisite for compliance, regulatory requirements affect the overall mission of the security department. This is not to suggest that regulations are exclusively negative. In fact, the presence of a government mandate can often strengthen the position of a security manager when recommending a program or specific countermeasure. When assessing the regulatory climate, ask yourself the following questions:

1. Does the regulatory environment affect both sides equally?

2. Which side has the most experience in effectively managing these issues?

3. Which side has the requisite resources already in place?

4. Which side is in a better overall position to respond to the mandate?

Responding to government mandates is a necessary part of the business world. Those organizations and departments that can effectively manage the compliance process are better positioned to be competitive than those that struggle with meeting minimum requirements.

- **Public relations issues**

The side with the most skillful public relations capability has a distinct advantage in today's media-centric world. Whether the specific scenario takes place on the macro business or an individual departmental level, the ability to shape the content and delivery of one's message to a mass audience has obvious appeal. Security managers need to have a fundamental understanding of public relations and how they affect the environment.

When assessing which side has the best public relations capability, the security professional needs to ask some basic questions:

1. Which side has the clearer message?

2. Which side has a more positive reputation?

3. Which side has the most access to the media in question?

4. Which side has had the most success dealing with these issues in the past?

By taking the time to examine these factors, the security professional can assess which side has the superior public relations position, whether dealing with inter- or intrabusiness conflicts.

- **External political, religious, and other controversial issues**

Conventional thinking holds that the subjects of politics, religion, and other controversial issues shouldn't be discussed in polite company, much less in the world of business. This short-sighted view ignores the fact that political, religious, and other controversial matters impact every facet of human life. Only in America are we so blinded by our "enlightenment" as to believe that these issues should be ignored. Just try doing business in the Middle East or Southeast Asia without feeling the impact of politics or religion! The fact is that it is impossible for an individual or organization to please everyone. Those who try waste resources on impossible objectives and lose credibility in the long run. The prepared organization knows where it stands and has plans to respond to the issues of the day.

When assessing the preparedness of an organization to respond to controversial issues, the security professional should ask the following questions:

1. Is the issue in question of importance to the organization?

2. Does the organization have a position on the issue?

3. Do management and employees support the firm's position?

4. Are plans in place to advance the firm's position?

5. Is management willing to make the "right" enemies to advance its position?

These questions and ones like them will provide the security professional with a means of determining who is better prepared to respond to the controversial issues of the day.

Terrain: Sun Tzu noted that military commanders should assess terrain in terms of ease or difficulty of travel (Cleary). Terrain, in this context, refers to the field of battle or conflict, whereas weather refers to the factors that influence our use of the field. When security managers use the term *terrain*, it could apply to our

1. Operational environment

2. Organizational risk tolerance

3. Historical and cultural factors

- **Operational environment**

Understanding the operational environment of a department or organization is critical to assessing the terrain. The operational environment can include the structure and mission of the organization, the available resources, internal political clout, policies, procedures, and a host of other factors that will influence how things get accomplished.

When assessing the operational environment, the security professional should ask the following questions:

1. Which side has a more clearly defined mission?

2. Which side has the most support of its constituent organization?

3. Which side has an organizational structure that is more conducive to accomplishing its mission?

4. Which side has the requisite resources to carry out the mission?

5. Which side has superior tactics, policies, and procedures in place?

- **Organizational risk tolerance**

Some element of risk is inherent in both life and business. Knowing an organization or department's level of tolerance to identified risks is important to assessing the terrain.

When assessing the risk tolerance of an organization or department, the security professional should ask the following questions:

1. Which side has conducted a comprehensive assessment of its assets, potential loss events and impacts, threats, risks, and vulnerabilities?

2. Which side has implemented reasonable countermeasures to mitigate its risks?

3. Which side has the most to gain from taking risks?

4. Which side has the most to lose from taking risks?

5. Which side's culture values risk taking more?

Security professionals who ask these questions and ones like them will be better informed as to the organizational risk tolerances of their own group and that of their adversary.

- **Historical and cultural factors**

The historical and cultural background of a department or organization is of critical importance to the assessment of terrain. Just as people's behavior is significantly influenced by personal background and culture, so, too, is the behavior of organizations.

The security professional should ask the following questions when assessing how history and culture will affect the decisions of the organization:

1. What previous patterns of behavior are suggested by each organization's history?

2. What cultural norms and mores are present for each side?

Leadership: Leadership in Sun Tzu's time and leadership today are not all that different. While it is true that the stakes of leading soldiers into battle are significantly higher than leading a business, the concepts of leadership are remarkably similar. Sun Tzu indicated that successful leaders must be intelligent, courageous, trustworthy and humane (Cleary). The same is true today. Generally, employees do what is expected of and modeled for them. A leader who consistently demonstrates the above referenced qualities will engender the respect of his or her employees, while still keeping the mission focused.

When assessing the leadership of an organization the following areas should be examined:

1. Experience

2. Expertise

3. Authority

4. Charisma

5. Weaknesses

- **Which side has the most experienced leadership?**

Experienced leadership is a key factor in any conflict. The side that has the most experienced leadership will, by definition, have a greater reservoir of applied knowledge, including previous mistakes and successes. The side with the least experienced leaders will be drawing from a shallow well of experience and will, in fact be experimenting at critical times.

- **Which side's leadership has the most expertise?**

In the course of any conflict there will be particular situations that require a focused expertise beyond normal operations. The side that has the expertise which is most relevant to the situation at hand has a distinct advantage.

- **Which sides' leadership exercises authority better?**

The proper exercise of authority is exceptionally important when leading an army, business or department. The side with the superior leadership is the one whose leaders use their authority for the greater good of the organization. The leader who uses authority properly is ethical. He does not seek personal glory because he understands that he is a servant of the organization, his commanders, and those under his command. As a result he is mission focused and does not favor personal comfort over the good of the group.

- **Which leader is more charismatic?**

There are times in every conflict when morale is low, the situation difficult, and the future appears bleak. In these situations the group can disintegrate if not properly led. The side whose leaders have the greater ability to motivate the troops are at an advantage.

- **Which leader has greater exploitable weaknesses?**

Leaders are human beings and, as such are vulnerable to human weaknesses. Impetuous leaders make unnecessarily bold moves that can endanger the group. Fearful leaders can be too cautious and miss opportunities. Leaders prone to anger can allow the adversary and internal situations to color his judgment. Leaders who seek personal glory are likely to forget the mission. Arrogant leaders are unlikely to admit vulnerabilities. When assessing the leadership of an organization it is vital to identify these potential weaknesses. Those leaders with the most easily identifiable and exploitable weaknesses are likely to lead their organization to ruin if left unchecked.

The side with the superior leadership is, not coincidentally, often the side with other strategic factors in their favor. In order to adequately assess the leadership of the organization, the security professional should focus on the aforementioned factors.

Discipline: Sun Tzu noted that the army with the most consistent and understandable system of rewards and punishments was in a better position than the army that was inconsistent or arbitrary in dealing with discipline issues (Cleary). As security professionals, we would do well to ask ourselves the same questions. Does our organization clearly define and consistently enforce policies and procedures? Does our organization reward people for going above and beyond their normal duties? Or, alternatively, do our employees not know what to expect from day to day?

When assessing the discipline of an organization, the following areas should be examined:

1. Clear chains of command

2. Clearly defined processes

3. Clearly defined and consistently enforced rules

4. Clear criteria for rewarding performance

5. Clear criteria for dealing with problems

- **Clear chains of command**

Chain of command is important for every organization. Unfortunately, many organizations do not have a clear chain of command. As a result employees either become confused or take advantage of this apparent lack of oversight. Simple chains of command work best because they mitigate confusion and establish a clear pathway for the flow of information. Where possible an individual should report to one manager or supervisor. When assessing chains of command the security professional should ask the following questions:

1. Which side has the simplest chain of command?

2. Which side's chain of command allows for the easiest communication pathway?

The answers to these and like questions will inform the security professional as to which side has the most efficient chain of command.

- **Clearly defined processes**

Every organization must have clearly defined processes for accomplishing core functions. Efficient processes are those that are easy to understand, high quality, fast, and consistent. Organizations that have clear, easy to understand processes with the fewest number of exceptions are the organizations that have a clear advantage. When assessing which side has superior processes the security professional should ask the following questions:

1. Which side's processes are easiest to understand?

2. Which side's processes are more consistent?

3. Which side's processes yield the highest quality in the shortest period of time?

The answers to these and like questions will inform the security professional as to which side has most clearly defined processes.

- **Clearly defined and consistently enforced rules**

Rules are necessary to the governance of all organizations. The effectiveness of a rule is determined by two factors: its clear definition and its consistent enforcement. When assessing which side has the most clearly defined and enforced rules the security professional should ask himself the following questions:

1. Are the rules simple to understand?

2. Are the rules communicated to all members of the organization?

3. Are the rules consistently enforced regardless of personal relationship or position?

The answers to these and like questions will inform the security professional as to which side has the most clearly defined and enforced rules.

- **Clear criteria for rewarding performance**

All organizations have expectations of their employees. When employees meet the expectations of their role they are rewarded according to their normally defined salary and benefit levels. When employees go above and beyond these expectations it is wise for the leadership to reward employees beyond the normally defined criteria. By doing so, the leadership encourages other employees to perform beyond expectations and over time raises the standard of the entire organization. When assessing which side has the best system of rewards the security professional should ask the following questions:

1. Are the basic compensation levels within industry norms?

2. Are the basic compensation levels sufficient for an employee to make a reasonable living?

3. Are basic expectations of all employees clearly defined and communicated?

4. Are the rewards for employees that go beyond expectations considered desirable by the widest possible base of employees?

5. Are rewards for going above expectations given out solely according to merit?

The answers to these and like questions will inform the security professional as to which side has the best system of rewards.

- **Clear criteria for dealing with problems**

All organizations must deal with personnel problems from time to time. The most successful organizations have clearly defined, consistently followed, and fair procedures. When evaluating an organization's criteria for dealing with discipline problems the security professional should ask the following questions:

1. Are all employees treated equally and consistently?

2. Do the procedures for dealing with discipline issues focus on the behavior in question?

3. Do the procedures allow for the development and execution of performance improvement plans?

The answers to these and like questions will inform the security professional as to which side has the best system for dealing with discipline issues.

Conducting a Strategic Assessment

When conducting a strategic assessment, the Security Manager should review all the aforementioned items and ask himself the following questions:

- **"The Way"**: Which side is superior at cultivating a sense of mission and loyalty?
- **The Weather:** What external conditions will affect operations and who do they favor?
- **The Terrain:** Which side is better positioned to take advantage of the environment?
- **Leadership:** Which side has the more capable leadership?
- **Discipline:** Which side has a clearer system of rewards and punishments?

The mathematics of strategic assessment is clear. The side with the most strategic factors on its side will win. The side with the least strategic factors in its favor will lose. Just as Sun Tzu could determine who will win a battle by assessing the five factors noted above, so too can today's Security Manager assess who will win today's conflicts.

Chapter 5 Scenario

Conducting strategic assessments is a vital component of security management. Based on your experience, education, training, and reading of Chapter 3 apply Sun Tzu's strategic assessment process to the following three scenarios:

➢ Choose an external adversary that your organization faces and apply Sun Tzu's strategic assessment process. The major tenants of the process are labeled below.

1. The Way

2. The Weather

3. The Terrain

  4. The Leadership

  5. Discipline

> Choose an internal adversary that your department faces and apply Sun Tzu's strategic assessment process. The major tenants of the process are labeled below.

  1. The Way

  2. The Weather

  3. The Terrain

  4. The Leadership

  5. Discipline

> After taking appropriate personal security precautions, commensurate with your risks and vulnerabilities, go to a public place in an urban area. The location should be a place where people come and go with frequency, such as a bus depot, park, or train station. Utilize your experience as a security professional along with Sun Tzu's assessment process to answer the following questions:

  1. What are the likely risks in this area? Why?

  2. Who are the likely threats in this area? Why?

  3. Who or what are the likely targets? Why?

  4. How does the physical layout of the location contribute or detract from personal security?

  5. What external conditions contribute or detract from personal security?

  6. Overall, how does Sun Tzu's strategic assessment process relate to personal security?

  7. Are there other scenarios you can think of where Sun Tzu's strategic assessment could be applied? If so, what are they?

Discussion Questions

  1. What are the differences between strategy and tactics?

  2. As a security professional, what types of circumstances necessitate the conduct of a strategic assessment?

  3. How often and under what circumstances, do we, as individuals conduct strategic assessments?

4. How do you or your organization attempt to cultivate "The Way"? Have these attempts been successful? If not, why?

5. Patrick Henry, while urging his fellow Virginians to enter into the American Revolution, remarked, "The battle is not to the strong alone, it is to the vigilant, the active the brave." Do you think this quote agrees with Sun Tzu's overall characterization of strategic assessments? Why or why not?

6 *Remember What Is Really Important*

So the important thing in a military operation is victory, not persistence.
Sun Tzu

Executive Summary

Neither the monikers of progressive and value-added nor the positions of comfort and familiarity form the basis of an effective strategy. Those who hold onto favorite processes, business models, techniques, or ideas that no longer match the reality of the environment will fail in their mission. Those who embrace new ideas for the sake of newness will also fail.

Security managers and other leaders who wish to remain relevant and vital to the organizations they serve will keep asking and answering the fundamental questions.

1. What is really important to the organization?
2. How does my department support those priorities?
3. How do other departments support those priorities?
4. How do I personally support those priorities?
5. What are my personal priorities and do they match the overall goals of the organization I serve?

The Schoolyard

In 1985, I witnessed two of my high school classmates get into a physical altercation. The physical initiator of the conflict wildly charged toward his adversary. As an onlooker, it was obvious that the attacker had no formal training in defensive tactics or martial arts. He was simply enraged and was focusing all of his energy toward the target of his aggression. The defender, by contrast, went into a perfect back stance and then executed a jumping side kick toward the attacker. The kick was technically perfect, except for one critical component; it didn't hit the attacker. The attacker temporarily slowed his advance to avoid the kick. When the defender landed, again in his perfect stance, the attacker charged forward. The defender once again executed a beautiful jumping side kick that failed to hit the target. The attacker again slowed his advance until the defender had landed, at which point he charged forward. The defender, predictably, executed yet another jumping side kick. This time, however, the attacker side stepped the kick, grabbed his leg and threw the defender to the ground. Once the defender was on the ground, the attacker jumped on top of him and started striking him repeatedly. Fortunately for both parties, neither person was seriously injured and school officials broke up the fight.

As I look back with some twenty years of life experience behind me, I have some questions about this incident:

1. What did the defender do, if anything, that made the attacker so angry?

2. Could this have been defused non-violently?

3. Why did the defender attempt to execute such an extraordinarily difficult technique in a real confrontation? After all, just because Chuck Norris can do it in the movies doesn't mean a 17-year-old can do it in real life.

4. Was this a failure of instruction? Did the defender's instructor not tell him how difficult the technique was to deliver in real life? Did he not tell him how to avoid physical conflict altogether?

5. When the technique failed the first time, why did the defender attempt it two more times? Was it the heat of the moment? Was it inexperience? Was he trying to show off for those around him?

I can only conjecture on some of these questions, but there is one clear lesson that is to be learned from this incident: ***Superior talent can be thwarted by one's own stubbornness!***

Sun Tzu's dictum that "*. . . the important thing in a military operation is victory, not persistence*" (Cleary) is of critical importance here. While this concept may seem obvious to most people, it is only obvious in an intellectual sense. The average person may understand the inherent logic of the statement. They may even be able to apply the logic when examining the actions of others, but the real test of knowledge is the personal application of the material to a real life situation. On that score, many otherwise intelligent people become so focused on the accomplishment of a particular objective, such as throwing a perfect jumping side kick, that they forget the overall objective—victory. If the defender in the incident above had not been so blinded by his apparent desire to show off, the outcome of the event would have been markedly different.

Okay, so a couple of kids got into a fight. One was committed to an ineffectual defensive technique and paid the price for his mistake. Certainly adults would be more mature than to make that same mistake, right? Well, not necessarily, and here is just one of many historical examples.

The Battlefield

In the years immediately following the first World War, France erected a large and complex fortification along its border with Germany. The fortification, known as the Maginot Line, was designed to offset Germany's numerical military advantage and buy time for the French military to mobilize against a German invasion force (American Heritage WWII).

The thinking behind the design of the Maginot Line was based on Frances' experiences during the first World War. During World War I, fortifications and trenches played a vital role in slowing the enemy's advance. It was thought that the construction of an "impenetrable" defensive position along the border would secure France's future. In 1936, Belgium abrogated its mutual defense treaty with France and declared neutrality. Having lost its ally to the north, France responded by making efforts to extend the line across the Belgian border. Unfortunately for France, time constraints, money and the geographic features of the area made the line much weaker in these new locations than they were at the sites of the original fortifications. In 1940, Germany invaded France via the low lands of Belgium and Holland, thus avoiding the strongest points of the Maginot Line (American Heritage WWII).

Lessons Learned

1. **Lighting doesn't strike twice:** While a historical analysis of past conflicts is important to strategic decision-making, it is equally important to realize that events never happen in quite the same way twice. France placed extensive reliance on strategies of the last major conflict to secure

her future. Blitzkrieg warfare involved significantly more speed, which was made possible by mechanization and the support of air power as well as the use of airborne troops to avoid the line altogether.

2. **Remember to follow through:** Contrary to popular belief, France *did* extend the Maginot Line, as well as the Alpine Line, across its entire border. The problem wasn't so much with the length of the defenses as with their quality. The extension of the Maginot Line along the Belgian border was not an original design feature, but occurred as a result of a broken alliance. When the line was extended, it appears that a German invasion through the lowlands was either thought unlikely to occur or likely to take longer than it actually did.

Just as the defender in our first example kept utilizing a favorite, though ineffective, technique to protect himself, so too did France utilize a familiar and ineffective technique to protect itself from the invading German army. While the scales of the conflicts are worlds apart, the mistakes stem from the same cause: being too persistent about utilizing a specific means of defense and, in the process, forgetting about the overall goal.

Equally as dangerous as the organization that holds onto outdated and ineffective processes and ideas is the organization that embraces new ideas and initiatives at the expense of its core mission. While at first glance these may seem like opposite problems, they, in fact, have the same cause: failing to remember what is really important!

The Business World

A computer firm in the Northeast had a large and well-established security department with multiple specialized groups. One group, responsible for day-to-day security operations, introduced a value-added program that deployed a corporate security representative as a liaison with each major business line. The program was an immediate success. The business lines enjoyed having a specific point of contact within the corporate security department. The liaison representatives enjoyed the professional opportunities to influence business line decisions, and the security department itself became an even more respected internal business partner. Similar value-added programs were added to each of the security department's functional groups. These programs were similarly received.

As time passed, the security department's managers and employees became very attached to the value-added programs—so much so, in fact, that there was some minor slippage in the performance levels of the core functions of the department. As long as economic times were going well, no one seemed to notice these problems. However, when an economic downturn occurred a few years later, the firm's senior management decided to reorganize several support functions and eliminate positions deemed nonessential.

The security department, with its large number of value-added programs, came under close scrutiny. This scrutiny revealed some performance issues and resulted in several people being laid off or transferred into security-related functions that were considered more core-oriented. Within a few months, many of those who had been transferred began to leave the firm. As people left, the security department's overall level of experience diminished and performance suffered as well.

The lesson to be drawn here is not that value-added programs are dangerous, but that value-added needs to be just that: core mission *plus* extra value. The security department that focuses on extra services at the expense of core missions will eventually find itself unable to effectively serve the organization.

What Really Matters?

The Organization

What is really important to your organization? Most of the time, you can forget about mission statements, slogans, and the other empty trappings of the corporate world. It's not that mission statements are a bad idea; on the contrary, if successfully assimilated into the corporate culture they can provide a model of what success is supposed to look like. Unfortunately, it is the exceedingly rare organization that continually makes the connection between ideals and operations. More typically, the fanciful language contained in mission statements become enshrined as wall decorations that have nothing to do with what is really valued by the organization.

While every enterprise is different, there are a number of key issues that are important to every organization:

- **Money:** Lets face it, the fundamental purpose of every business is to generate revenue for the shareholders. This statement is true whether one is speaking of a small diner or a large multinational conglomerate. Even non-profit organizations must generate revenue in the form of donations to stay solvent. As a result of the key role that money plays, security managers, especially at senior levels, must possess a solid understanding of financial matters and how they affect the overall performance of the firm.

- **New business opportunities:** Market conditions change quickly. Successful organizations are quick to seize opportunities. The successful security manager must always understand and accept the fact that opportunities to generate revenue will always take precedence over security matters. In executive management's view, it is the responsibility of the security manager and other risk management professionals to design protections around the business and not vice versa. The rare exceptions to this rule are extreme circumstances where the expense of mitigation is prohibitive and the potential risks, vulnerabilities, and impacts are so great that they will cost lives and destroy the firm.

- **Reputation:** We live in an age of democratized mass media. Although large television and radio networks as well as newspapers, books, and magazines are still quite influential, the Internet has expanded the proverbial public soap box. Anyone with online access and a small bit of technical knowledge can publish a blog with running commentary on virtually any topic. This democratization of the media has exponentially increased the power of individuals to influence consumer behavior. The successful security manager must possess some knowledge of how the media can affect the reputation of the organization.

- **Vital processes:** Every organization has processes by which it accomplishes its purpose or purposes. A process is composed of several tasks and supported by personnel, equipment, and supplies. A process may touch one or multiple departments within the organization. A *vital* process is one that must be accomplished in order for the organization to continue to exist. Typically, a vital business process has either very low or zero periods of acceptable downtime. The successful security manager must have an understanding of the vital processes so that adequate protection measures can be designed and executed. He or she need not be an expert on all of the vital processes, but should go to great lengths to work with business lines and other support functions.

- **Regulatory environment:** Every industry has some type of government regulation, standard, guideline industry best practice, or legal precedent that impacts its ability to do business. Since failure to comply with these can result in fines, damage to the organization's reputation, and, in some cases, day-to-day operations, the organization must keep abreast of the regulatory environment and at a minimum maintain compliance. Since several of these requirements have to do with safety and security matters, the successful security manager needs to have a solid understanding of these requirements and the ability to obtain assistance when needed.

When evaluating what is valuable to your organization, ask yourself:

1. What are the purpose, goals, and/or mission of the organization?

2. What reputational risks does your organization face?

3. What new business opportunities are most likely to serve the organization's purposes?

4. What vital processes need to occur in order to accomplish the organization's purposes?

5. What regulatory issues are likely to affect your firm?

The Department

What is really important to your department? This question is of vital importance to the security manager because it drives, or should drive, all activities that the department undertakes. In many security departments, objectives are driven not by what is important but by what has always been done in the past or what the department happens to be good at. This mode of operation is dangerous because it can ignore changing organizational conditions that will impact the nature of the department's mission.

Although every security department is unique, a number of key issues are important to all departments:

- **Support of organizational goals:** The overall goal of the security department is to help manage risks so that the enterprise can be profitable. All too often, security managers lose sight of this important fact and start to confuse the means by which their department contributes to the organization with the goals of the department. Security departments *do not* exist to catch criminals. Although investigating crimes and violations of company policy is one of the *means* by which the security department contributes to the organization, it is not the overall *goal*. Even the police *do not* exist to catch criminals; the police exist to maintain order. Catching criminals is simply the *means* by which they accomplish the overall *goal* of order. The successful security manager will always keep this in mind. Those who don't learn this lesson will not be able to serve their organization appropriately and will eventually burn out from frustration.

- **Security as a business partner:** The security department can contribute to the firm's pursuit of new business opportunities in several ways. These include preacquisition due diligence and risk/vulnerability

assessments, as well as countermeasure development and project implementation, to name just a few. The successful security manager will
take steps to ensure that security is considered an internal business
partner. By linking security with the organization's pursuit of new
opportunities, the security department will become more important to
the organization. As a result, the organization will be more resilient
and more profitable.

- **Reputation:** The security department can contribute to the positive
  reputation of the organization in both big and small ways. The security
  officer is generally the first person the customer or visitor sees when
  entering the facility. If the security officer is professional in knowledge,
  demeanor, and appearance, this will enhance the overall impression of
  the organization. If the security officer does not appear professional,
  this too will influence the visitor's impression of the organization.
  Beyond simple first impressions, the security department impacts the
  organization's reputation in the way it carries out its duties. If the
  security department consistently seeks to maintain high standards of
  professionalism, it is more likely to respond to both critical and day-
  to-day incidents in ways that management, the media, law enforcement, and the public view as reasonable. The successful security
  manager will ensure that all levels and types of security personnel are
  properly selected, managed, and developed in such a way as to enhance
  the organization's goals and reputation.

- **Protection of vital interests and assets:** When the word "security"
  comes to mind, many people think of the protection of the organization's assets. The security department can and does help to protect
  critical assets by maintaining access and property control, responding
  to emergencies, investigating losses, and raising awareness. In addition,
  progressive security departments also contribute through active participation in planning for and implementing countermeasures for vital
  business processes. In most critical incidents, it is the security personnel
  who first become aware of, respond to, and notify other groups of the
  emergency. The successful security manager will take steps to ensure
  that every person in his or her department understands both their specific duties and the overall context of why their duties are important.
  Beyond this, the security manager should ensure that business lines and
  other support groups understand the role of security in such incidents.

- **Regulatory environment:** Security departments can contribute to the
  organization's interest in maintaining regulatory requirements. This is
  often accomplished through patrol reports or hazardous conditions, as

well as inspections, participation in safety committees, and liaison with safety and other risk management professionals. The successful security manager will ensure that all personnel have at least a basic understanding of relevant regulatory requirements for their facility and industry. By serving as the eyes and ears of management, the security department can help the organization avoid fines, accidents, lawsuits, and public damage to the organization's reputation.

When evaluating what is valuable to your department, ask yourself:

1. Do the day-to-day and long-range goals of the security department directly support the goals of the organization?

2. Is there confusion between the goals of the department and the means of accomplishing the goals?

3. How does the security department support the acquisition of new business opportunities?

4. How does the security department protect the image and reputation of the organization?

5. How does the security department contribute to the protection of the vital business of the organization?

6. How does the security department assist in maintaining the organization's compliance with regulatory requirements?

The Security Manager

What is really important to you as a security professional? Just as the question of what is important to the organization and the department is of vital importance, so too is the question of what is important to you, the security professional. As a manager, you set the tone for your department. If your goals are congruent with those of the organization, then you can bring a unified momentum to the mission at hand. If the goals are not congruent, then your energy will be dissipated and inefficient.

Every individual has his or her own professional goals, but all security professionals should know the answers to the following questions:

1. **Do you believe in the organization's mission?** Managers who believe in the mission are more likely to align their own and their department's goals with those of the organization. Are you proud of the organization you work for, or is it just a job? Are you biding your time until something better comes along? Just as it is important for your employees to

have a sense of mission, it is equally important for you as well. If, despite your best efforts, you can't bring yourself to support the organization's mission, it may be time to look at employment in another organization where you are more committed.

2. **Do you see yourself as a business manager as well as a security manager?** The days of just being a security manager are long gone. Today's security professionals need to have knowledge not only of security, but of business, information technology, safety, business continuity, training, and regulatory requirements, to name just a few. The more broad-based security managers can be, while still maintaining an area of expertise, the more successful and happy they will be.

3. **How important is the organization's and your own reputation?** Ethics are paramount in the security profession, and it is generally assumed that if you've chosen security as your profession, then ethics are important to you. Do you consider the organization you work for to be ethical? If not, do you have the power to change those aspects of the organization that are ethically wrong or questionable? If not, then you have to consider what is more important to you—your job, or your career? your current financial status, or your personal integrity?

4. **Do you want to try new things, or are you content with the way things are?** Security today is not for the faint of heart. While some organizations still are the same day after day, most organizations change regularly and radically. Security managers who can change with the organizational and market conditions will be successful and content. Those who cannot will be unhappy and frustrated. Remember, we spend more time at work than anywhere else. You owe it to yourself and your family to be joyful and content.

5. **How do you view compliance and regulatory issues?** Like it or not, government regulations, industry standards, and such are part of life for a security manager. If you view compliance with laws, regulations, and standards as tedious and unimportant, then so will your staff. If your staff doesn't view these issues as important, then that part of your department's mission will fail.

Victory Is Important, Not Persistence

The security manager who understands and supports what is important to the organization will be better suited to determine and direct the goals and objectives of the security department. Holding on to tradition for tradition's

Figure 6-1   *Programs and goals of each element of risk management must align with organizational goals and needs.*

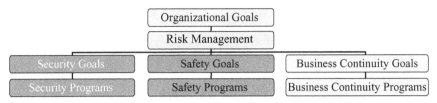

sake or taking on new and exciting programs while abandoning aspects of the core mission will result in disaster.

Remember what is *not* important:

1. Doing what you've always done because it's what you've always done.

2. Taking on new and exciting projects simply because they are new and exciting.

3. Getting caught up in exciting projects and forgetting about core missions.

4. Your personal glory.

Remember what *is* important: efficiently utilizing resources to accomplish the mission, while maintaining a high degree of integrity and professionalism.

Chapter 6 Scenario

Pick any organization to which you belong. The organization could be your work, your church, your civic group, or any other type of organization. Based on the material in this chapter, review the organization and draw some conclusions about what is really important to the organization.

1. What is really important to _____?

2. Why are these things really important? On what do you base these conclusions?

3. Does the organization have a mission statement? If so, does the mission statement resemble your conclusions?

4. Are your personal goals congruent with those of the organization? Why or why not?

Discussion Questions

1. Describe a situation in which someone or some organization continued to use an ineffective technique or tool to accomplish the mission.

2. Why do you think that people hold on to what is comfortable even when it appears to be ineffective?

3. Why do you think that people who take on new responsibilities will sometimes ignore their old responsibilities? As a security manager, how would you prevent this from occurring?

4. What steps can you take to ensure that your department's goals are aligned with the organization's goals?

5. Does the following statement surprise you? Do you agree with it? Why or why not?

   Security departments *do not* exist to catch criminals. While investigating crimes and violations of company policy is one of the *means* by which the security department contributes to the organization, it is not the overall *goal*. Even the police *do not* exist to catch criminals. The police exist to maintain order. Catching criminals is simply the *means* by which they accomplish the overall *goal* of order.

7 *Engage the Enemy*

The superior militarist strikes while schemes are being laid. The next best is to attack alliances. The next best is to attack the army. The lowest is to attack a city. Siege a city only as a last resort.

Sun Tzu

Executive Summary

To engage and prevail in battle requires the alignment of key factors. This chapter examines the following such factors.

1. Solid preparation

2. Skill assessment

3. Creation of "invincibility" in oneself and one's organization

4. Discovery of the vulnerability of one's adversary

5. Understanding of the battle equation

6. The judicious application of force against weakness.

Preparations

You have taken the time to establish yourself as a leader. You understand that conflict is inevitable. You have held up the magnifying glass to your own organization and to yourself as a leader. As a result of this introspection, you know yourself. You are neither arrogant and overconfident nor fearful and indecisive. You have studied your adversary. You understand your enemy's mission, organization, resources, and motivation. You know the enemy as well as you know yourself. You have conducted an assessment of the strategic factors in your favor and in favor of your adversary. The assessment leads you to believe that you will succeed. You know what is really important. You realize that the endeavor you are about to undertake is not about heroics or personal glory; it is about one thing and one thing only—victory. Rally the troops; it's time to engage the enemy.

The Context of Battle

So, does the thought of battle raise your blood pressure? Does your heart quicken? Do you feel the intoxicating flood of adrenaline surging through your body? If you are going into combat, you should feel all these things. It is how our bodies were designed. The parasympathetic nervous system engages us, and the overwhelming desire to fight or run takes over. Now, that's true if we're talking about actual combat, but we're talking about engaging the enemy in battle, and those two things are not necessarily the same.

Sun Tzu said, "The general rule for the use of the military is that it is better to keep a nation intact than to destroy it. It is better to keep an army intact than to destroy it, better to keep a division intact than to destroy it, better to keep a battalion intact than to destroy it, better to keep a unit intact than to destroy it" (Cleary) (p. 17).

Sun Tzu argued that the objective of warfare is not to utterly destroy the enemy because to attempt such a task is to needlessly put one's own forces, and indeed the nation itself, at risk of destruction. Rather, the goal of warfare is to achieve the nation's political objectives. The objective of a general is, therefore, to outthink and outmaneuver the enemy, to limit losses while keeping the sword of the nation sharp and the shield of the nation raised.

Sun Tzu continues the passage by stating: "Therefore those who win every battle are not really skillful—those who render other's armies helpless without fighting are the best of all" (Cleary).

This brings us to the opening quote on which this chapter is based. "The superior militarist strikes while schemes are being laid. The next best is to attack alliances. The next best is to attack the army. The lowest is to attack a city. Siege a city only as a last resort" (Cleary) (p. 18).

Types of Militarists

Sun Tzu clearly delineated a ranking system based on martial skill, as follows.

1. **The grandmaster militarist:** One who achieves a completely one-sided victory in which objectives are met without risk to one's own forces. Grandmaster militarists win by "striking" while the enemy lays out his schemes. In doing so, the grandmaster convinces the enemy that making war is not in his interest. He does this with such acumen that the enemy is not even aware that his plans were foiled by the grandmaster and instead blames internal adversaries, allies, or natural conditions for the failure of his schemes. The grandmaster always wins because he doesn't need to fight.

2. **The master militarist:** One who achieves victory with very little risk to one's own forces. Master militarists strike at the enemies' alliances. They cause division and strife among their adversaries and thus weaken their ability and motivation to make war. The master consistently wins because he positions himself in such a way as to ensure victory.

3. **The black belt:** One who achieves victory by successfully attacking the enemy's weak points and defeating the enemy in battle. Just as the modern martial arts generally consider a black belt to be a person who is proficient in the basics of a given fighting system, so, too, a black belt militarist is proficient in the basics of battle. He does not make obvious mistakes, but he still uses far more energy at far greater risk to his forces than does a master or grandmaster militarist. As a result of this greater risk, the black belt may lose many battles.

4. **The colored belts:** Those who achieve victory at exceptionally high risk to their own forces. Within the colored belts are several subgroups. At the highest level of the colored belts are those that have some knowledge of fighting, but aren't quite proficient enough to be a black belt yet. At the lowest level of the colored belts are the absolute beginners, with virtually no skills. The beginner is prone to letting anger and ego get the best of him. He consistently seeks personal glory over the mission and as a result of these factors wins only when his adversary is even more inept than himself.

So when we discuss engaging the enemy in battle, we must remember the fundamental truth that the word "battle" or "conflict" is significantly broader in scope and covers a greater number of arenas than does the word "combat." This understanding should serve to give you respect for the full range of options at your disposal.

Fundamental Concepts of Battle

When doing battle, the general has two basic strategies and countless tactics at his disposal. The two basic strategies are defense and attack. Sun Tzu said, "In ancient times skillful warriors first made themselves invincible, and then watched for vulnerability in their opponents. Invincibility is in oneself, vulnerability is in the opponent. Therefore skillful warriors are able to be invincible, but they cannot cause their opponents to be vulnerable. That is why it is said that victory can be discerned but not manufactured" (Cleary) (pp. 25–26).

Invincibility

When people think of invincibility in today's world, they tend to think of it in absolutes and casually dismiss the invincibility clause in the above statement. After all, who can truly be invincible? Everyone has a weakness, right? This is a fair criticism if one looks at Sun Tzu's statement from a contemporary Western analytical perspective. However, since Sun Tzu was neither a Westerner nor a contemporary of ours, the analytical Western viewpoint does not lend itself to a proper interpretation.

When Sun Tzu wrote of invincibility, he did so in the context of providing professional military instruction to professional military officers. As a result of this context, it is clear that the scope of Sun Tzu's views on invincibility applied directly to his work. When Sun Tzu wrote that "invincibility is in oneself" (Cleary), he was neither referring to contemporary humanist philosophy nor puffing up his students with feel-good slogans. Rather, he was reiterating the importance of following the rules of strategy. The invincible general, in this context, is the general who understands and consistently applies the rules of strategy.

In the security world, we often see this concept at work when conducting facility risk and vulnerability assessments. Can our facilities ever truly be invincible? No, they cannot. Unfortunately, the leadership of the organizations we serve often do not understand this concept. It is up to us as security professionals to educate them. Have you ever had an executive or client ask you if they were "vulnerable"? How did you answer?

My stock answer for this question is "Vulnerable to what? If the 82nd Airborne wants your building, they're going to get it. It is not a question of vulnerability, but of vulnerability in the context of a specific threat." The same is true for Sun Tzu's statement of invincibility.

Vulnerability

ASIS International's General Security Risk Assessment Guideline defines a security vulnerability as "An exploitable capability; an exploitable weakness or deficiency at a facility, entity, venue, or of a person" (ASIS) (p. 5). Sun Tzu viewed vulnerability as a weakness in the adversary. The successful general, after having made himself invincible, would then seek to find vulnerability in his adversary. The successful security manager, after having enhanced readiness within the scope of the organizational mission, threat profile, and available resources should seek vulnerabilities in his adversaries.

The Battle Equation

We can think of invincibility and vulnerability as two sides of an equation where:

I = Invincibility

V = Vulnerability

G = General

A = Adversary

and

Invincibility > Vulnerability

The ability of the general or security manager to thoroughly understand and consistently apply the rules of strategy is within his own power. This idea is the heart of Sun Tzu's concept of invincibility and is expressed here as:

$$(G + I) > V$$

The general is invincible because he has followed the rules of strategy and thus is not vulnerable.

The other side of the equation is not controlled by the general or security manager because neither can cause the adversary to ignore the rules of strategy. This notion is expressed here as:

$$(A + I) > V$$

The adversary is invincible because he has followed the rules of strategy and thus is not vulnerable. This equation, if balanced, creates an impasse where

$$(G + I) = (A + I)$$

In this case, both the general (G) and the adversary (A) are invincible (I). As a result, the equation is balanced with neither side having an advantage.

This is why Sun Tzu wrote that "victory can be discerned but not manufactured" (Cleary). The objective of the general or security manager is, therefore, to maintain control of his own side of the equation while waiting for the adversary to make a mistake by ignoring the rules of strategy. This would be expressed in our equation as:

$$(G + I) > (A + V)$$

In this case, the general (G) is invincible (I), but the adversary (A) is vulnerable (V). The result is that the equation is out of balance, giving advantage to the general.

Basic Battle Strategies

The two basic strategies of battle, as noted earlier, are defense and attack. Sun Tzu said, "Defense is for times of insufficiency. Attack is for times of surplus" (Cleary) (p. 26).

Defense

Defense is the strategy employed by those whose forces are smaller and resources less abundant. Defense is a matter of invincibility; in other words, the objective of the defender is simply to not be defeated. As a result of this objective, the defender has some advantages over the attacker.

1. The defender can retreat as long as he has an escape route. In contrast, the attacker must directly engage and defeat the defender in order to achieve victory.

2. The defender can avoid the attacker and still meet his objective. The attacker must find the defender, which takes energy and can spread his forces into smaller sizes whose component parts may themselves come under attack.

3. The defender can split his forces and make it even more difficult for the attacker to find him.

4. The defender can engage in harassment of the attacker by striking weak areas and then retreating. When this happens repeatedly, the morale of the attacker suffers while the morale of the defender increases.

5. The defender can gather human intelligence more easily than can the attacker because the relative size of the attacker creates more opportunities for leaks. By contrast, the attacker must first find the smaller force of the defender and then start to gather information.

Attack

The strategy of attack is for times when resources are in surplus. The reason for this is that it takes significantly more energy than it does to mount a defense. The objective of the attacker is to render the defender's forces useless by either convincing them to surrender, trapping them, critically damaging them, or destroying them in battle. Just as the defender has some advantages over the attacker, so too does the attacker have certain advantages.

1. The attacker has more resources and troop strength available than does the defender.

2. The attacker typically initiates the action and thus has the element of surprise on his side. The defender must react to the attack.

3. The attacker can operate in the open and move directly. The defender must hide and use circuitous routes of travel.

4. The attacker can cut off access to strategic areas by virtue of his superior resources.

5. The attacker can sustain more damage and still emerge victorious due to superior resources and strength.

Choosing a Basic Battle Strategy

When assessing what basic battle strategy to employ, the leader must ask the following questions:

1. What is my objective? Do I need to conquer, or is the objective simply to keep from being defeated?

2. What is my relative strength compared to that of my adversary?

3. What resources do I have at my disposal?

These three questions will give the leader a basic strategy. The application of the strategy will require an understanding of force and the use of both orthodox and unorthodox tactics.

Force

Force or strength is an often misunderstood element of battle. When the strongest elements of opposing forces collide, the result of the battle is dependent on whose strength is greater. While the side with the greater strength will win, the cost of victory may be high, especially if the sides have parity. If multiple battles need to be fought, the energy level of the army will be dispersed and any advantage of strength will be lost with time. This situation commonly occurs when the belligerents lack an understanding of the correct use of force. Contrary to what many people believe, the proper use of force is not against opposing force; rather, the correct use of force is against opposing weakness.

Sun Tzu illustrated this principle by using the analogy of emptiness and fullness. Sun Tzu said, "For the impact of armed forces to be like stones thrown on eggs is a matter of emptiness and fullness" (Cleary) (p. 33). In this illustration, emptiness can be equated with weakness and fullness with strength or force. Note that Sun Tzu did *not* say that force is to be likened to the impact of stones thrown against a brick wall. The lesson for leaders is clear, the successful side is the one that strikes when the odds are overwhelmingly in its favor and avoids contact when in weaker positions.

The following situations illustrate the correct use of force in several types of conflict:

1. **Physical assault:** A 250-pound man grabs a 110-pound woman by the wrist. Because of the disparity in their arm strength, the woman can't break free by forcing her arm against his. The woman responds by moving her entire arm against the weakest part of his grip, where the thumb and fingers meet. She breaks free and follows up with an elbow strike to the assailant's Adam's apple. The man retreats in breathless pain. The woman escapes to safety.

2. **Armed robbery:** A man wants to commit an armed robbery. He could choose to rob the local bank branch where it is commonly known that tellers are trained to cooperate with a robber's demands, or he could try to hold up an armored car staffed by armed guards. If he chooses the former, he will at least get to leave the premises safely. If he chooses the latter, he runs the risk of getting shot. The robber wisely chooses the bank branch.

3. **Laptop thief:** A man wants to steal laptop computers, purses, and wallets from a nearby office building. The building has two main entrances staffed by security personnel and a third entrance secured

by a card reader. The thief approaches the unstaffed entrance, lights a cigarette, and strikes up a conversation with employees who are taking a smoking break. Within a few minutes one of the employees puts out his cigarette and enters the facility. The thief follows the employee inside and proceeds to walk confidently through departments, stealing as he goes. He eventually leaves through the unprotected entrance through which he entered.

4. **Addition to staff:** A security manager is concerned about the possibility of a domestic violence incident occurring in the workplace. In order to mitigate this possibility, the security manager decides to add another officer to enhance perimeter protection. When making the case for the additional cost, the security manager could argue that the extra officer would help to mitigate the possibility of a domestic violence situation. If the manager makes this argument, he knows that at least some will contend that, since this has never happened before, there is no need for the additional officer. The security manager decides to frame the request for the additional officer as an attempt to mitigate the laptop thefts that have been occurring through the employee smoker's entrance. Since some of the recently stolen laptops belonged to managers, the security manager gets his additional officer.

5. **Mission expansion:** A security manager wants to expand his department's mission to include an executive protection function. The company has never had an executive protection program, and senior management is against the idea. The security manager could argue his point by providing senior management with case studies of horrific incidents, but that is likely to be seen as fear mongering. Instead, the security manager presents the idea slowly, over time. The security department starts to offer alarm monitoring at executives' homes as a value-added service. The security manager then suggests that a security receptionist be posted on the executive floor to free up the executive's administrative staff for other duties. The security manager offers travel information to senior managers on business trips. As this slow expansion of mission continues, as part of value-added services, senior management begins to warm to the idea of an executive program.

In each of these situations, force was applied against weakness in order to achieve an objective.

- The woman whose wrist was grabbed used the concentrated power of her entire arm against the weakest and most vulnerable areas of her assailant. Despite being in an overall weaker position, she prevailed by bringing the fullness of her power against the emptiness of his power.

- The robber focused his energies against the weakness of his victim. Instead of attempting to hold up an armored car staffed with armed guards, he used his power against the weaker target: unarmed and cooperative branch employees.

- The laptop thief avoided the protected entrances of the office building, blended in with the employees, and departed the facility through the same unprotected entrance he entered.

- The security manager who wanted an additional officer to enhance perimeter protection framed his question in such as way as to avoid criticism from management. Instead, he leveraged the concern over recent thefts to mitigate two risks.

- The security manager who wanted to establish an executive protection program avoided resistance by senior management. He slowly introduced value-added services, which were, in reality, some of the building blocks of an executive protection program. Over time, senior management began to rely on these services and warm to the idea of a formal program.

When engaging in battle, the security professional should be aware of the following elements:

1. **Preparation:** Have you established yourself as a leader? Do you understand that conflict is inevitable? Do you know yourself, your organization's capabilities, and the capabilities of your adversary? Have you conducted a comparative strategic assessment? Do you understand that victory and not persistence is important?

2. **Skill:** How skilled are you? Are you a grandmaster, master, black belt, or some level of colored belt?

3. **Strategy:** What is your objective, and how does that drive your battle strategy? Do you have surplus or insufficient resources?

4. **Invincibility:** Do you understand and consistently follow the rules of strategy?

5. **Vulnerability:** Do your opponent's vulnerabilities outweigh your own?

6. **Force:** Do you apply your strength against the adversary's weakness?

Chapter 7 Scenario

You have just been hired as the director of security for a software firm that has 250 employees spread across three sites. Prior to your arrival, the company had no corporate security program. The security apparatus that was in place was focused solely on network security issues. Senior management has defined the scope of your responsibilities as head of physical security of the three properties. After spending a few months in your new position, you see a need for an expansion of the department's mission to include internal investigations. Describe how you would go about establishing the need for such a program. How would you overcome objections?

Discussion Questions

1. What, in your experience, distinguishes various levels of martial skill?

   Grandmaster

   Master

   Black belt

   Colored belts

2. Describe what it means to be invincible in the context of this chapter?

3. What is vulnerability, and how does it apply to your job?

4. What is better skilled weakness or unskilled strength? Why?

5. What does "victory can be discerned but not manufactured" mean?

靈活機動

8 *Maneuver Your Army*

The terrain is to be assessed in terms of distance, difficulty or ease of travel, dimension, and safety.
Sun Tzu

Executive Summary

Maneuverability and the use of terrain are of vital importance to the successful conduct of military operations, security operations, and business decisions. This chapter applies Sun Tzu's discussion of terrain and mobility to everyday situations that can be faced by the security professional.

Sun Tzu's *Act of War* describes six types of terrain (Cleary) that the general or security manager must understand in order to maneuver his army or department. The types of terrain include:

1. Easily passable terrain

2. Hung-up terrain

3. Standoff terrain

4. Narrow terrain

5. Steep terrain

6. Wide-open terrain

Conflicts are not static. Armies, organizations, and individuals must be maneuverable in order to gain positions that are advantageous to their interests. In warfare, terrain and position play a vital role in determining victory or defeat. Sun Tzu outlined the concepts of terrain and maneuverability in *The Art of War* and documented a series of rules that were to be followed by officers. These rules apply to military and other types of conflict to this day.

As security professionals, we must understand that, for us, terrain will most often apply to the organizational environment. Occasionally, depending on the type of security in which we are engaged, the more military aspects of terrain will be applicable to our situation.

Terrain and Position

Sun Tzu identified six types of terrain (Cleary).

1. **Easily passable terrain:** This terrain is easy to move through and by itself offers no particular advantage to either side. In order to gain advantage in easily passable terrain, Sun Tzu said, "When the terrain is easily passable, take up your position first, choosing the high and sunny side, convenient to supply routes, for advantage in battle" (Cleary) (p. 80).

   As a security manager, you, too, may find yourself in terrain that is easily passable for both yourself and your adversary. By taking the initiative and seizing the best position first, you can gain a positional advantage. This is why it is sometimes wise to expand the protective perimeter of a facility when protesters or other hostile actors are expected to approach the facility.

2. **Hung-up terrain:** This type of terrain is characterized by the difficulty of getting back to your original position if things do not turn out as expected.

   As a security manager, it is important for you to avoid situations where everything is committed to one position or course of action. If security managers attempt a specific course of action, they must have contingencies. If they do not have contingencies in place and the plan fails badly, security managers will make their superiors question the course of action, the manager's competency, and in some cases, the mission itself.

3. **Standoff terrain:** Standoff terrain occurs when it is in neither side's interest to venture forth. As a security manager, it is possible to find yourself positioned in standoff terrain. Typically, this occurs when a regulatory requirement or corporate policy mandates the presence of a certain program but fails to address the quality of the program as expressed in specific measurements. In this case, an adversary of the program will be compelled to participate, but will do so in a nominal manner. As a result, nothing really gets accomplished.

4. **Narrow terrain:** Narrow terrain can occur in a mountain pass or other areas where there is little room for maneuverability. Sun Tzu advised,

"If you are there first you should fill it up to await the opponent. If the opponent arrives first do not pursue if the opponent fills up the narrows" (Cleary) (p. 81). The rationale behind this principle is that the army who fills in the narrow terrain is able to concentrate the strongest part of its force toward its enemy and take advantage of the natural barriers surrounding the site of battle.

As a security manager, you should avoid attacking the position of an adversary who controls narrow terrain. Narrow terrain in this context can take the form of corporate traditions that may have potentially negative security consequences, such as labeled and reserved parking spaces. These traditions may be so well entrenched that a direct attack will cost you more than is likely to be gained. If you commit to this course of action, you may be able to retreat from it, but not without significant cost.

5. **Steep terrain:** Steep terrain, like narrow terrain and hung-up terrain, offers clear advantages to the side that arrives first. As a security manager, you must be quick to seize the high ground.

   When a new issue that has security implications presents itself, the security department must act immediately. Failure to do so may result in another group creating a solution that is unworkable from a security perspective. If this occurs, the security manager will be in a weak position to change the already existing protocol. The successful security manager must therefore keep abreast of new products, services, and programs that are likely to have a security impact.

6. **Wide-open terrain:** Wide-open terrain creates a situation in which both sides are completely exposed. As a result, it is difficult to mount an attack because the features of the landscape do not provide cover. In a military sense, if a side has significantly greater numbers, it can successfully engage the enemy, but will still suffer a high number of casualties.

Security managers who find themselves on wide-open terrain should not try to mount an attack but should instead maneuver their department into a better position. This may be accomplished by attempting to reframe the issue, waiting for the adversary to make a mistake, or withdrawing into familiar and advantageous territory.

Rules for Maneuvering Armies

Sun Tzu created a number of rules for the maneuverability of armies (Cleary), including:

1. *"When fighting on a hill do not climb"* (Cleary) (p. 67). Why make your mission more difficult by trying to advance uphill onto fortified positions? The successful security manager will seek to accomplish his mission by utilizing energy efficiently.

2. *"When cut off from the water do not meet them in the water, always stay away from the water; it is advantageous to let half of them cross and then attack them"* (Cleary) (p. 67). The general who avoids getting his forces trapped while simultaneously inducing the adversary to compromise his position will be successful. Similarly, the security manager needs to avoid the traps of underestimating his adversaries and becoming complacent.

3. *"Go right through salt marshes, just go quickly and do not tarry"* (Cleary) (p. 68). There are times when an army will be exposed to attack. The general should ensure that those times are limited as much as possible. The security manager must also ensure that exposures are limited.

4. *"Take up position where it is easy to maneuver"* (Cleary) (p. 68). The general must ensure that his forces are positioned in such a way as to make movement easy. The security manager must ensure that he or she has several options open, whether dealing with an operational security threat or an internal competitor.

5. *"Those who come seeking peace without a treaty are plotting"* (Cleary) (p. 73). Leaders must constantly compare the stated aims of their adversaries with their actions. In cases where the stated aims differ from actions, the leader needs to be extra vigilant.

6. *"If half of their force advances and half retreats, they are trying to lure you"* (Cleary) (p. 74). The general must be wary of attempts to lure his forces into a trap. Similarly, the security manager must observe his or her adversary's actions in order to ascertain whether they make sense given the circumstance. Assuming the adversary is a rational actor, this observation will inform the security manager's decisions.

7. *"When they see an advantage but do not advance on it, they are weary"* (Cleary) (p. 74). An adversary that fails to follow up on your mistakes is either inept or tired. If you judge the adversary to be tired, it is time to attack.

Movement

When assessing the direction in which to maneuver your department, the following questions should be asked.

1. What type of terrain am I on? In other words, what is your department's operational environment?

2. Which side does the terrain favor? Are you in a favorable position?

3. Should I wait for the adversary to move first? Is your best advantage to wait and see what move your competitor/opponent makes first?

4. Is my movement impeded? Are there factors that keep your department from acting?

5. Can I take circuitous routes to confuse the enemy? Is there an indirect path to achieve your department's objectives?

6. Can I take advantage of the natural features of the terrain? What is it about your organization's environment that favors your department?

7. Does withdrawing place me in a better position? Can you yield on a specific point now, in order to advance your overall objective?

8. Can I induce the adversary to come to me? How can you lure your competitor or opponent into making a careless error?

9. Can I tire the adversary by creating the appearance of movement? Is your security department being proactive in its deployment of personnel and its use of resources?

10. Can I entice the enemy to split its forces? Do the strategies and tactics of your security department cause your adversary to divide its resources?

By asking these questions and questions like them, the general will be able to accurately assess the dynamic changes to the field of battle and the security manager will be able to ascertain the proper direction of movement for his or her department.

Chapter 8 Scenario

Assume, hypothetically, that a former employee has threatened to harm you. Conduct a security analysis of the path you take to and from work. What impact does the terrain have on your personal safety? In what areas of the route are you most vulnerable? Other than changing and mixing up routes, what can be done to mitigate the risk of attack?

Discussion Questions

1. Why is maneuverability important in military operations?

2. In Chapter 2, we discussed the battle of Thermopylae as an illustration of leadership. Review the description of the battle from Chapter 2 and any other sources you have on the event and describe how terrain played a pivotal role in the outcome.

3. Why is maneuverability important to business world conflicts?

4. Describe a personal or professional situation where maneuverability made the difference between success and failure.

5. Why is withdrawing from the field sometimes the best course of action?

6. Why is it important to be the first to arrive at the site where you intend to do battle?

9 *Adapt to the Battlefield*

*The unorthodox and the orthodox give rise to each other, like a
beginningless circle—who could exhaust them?*

Sun Tzu

Executive Summary

Adaptation is a key element for every manager, leader, and security professional. Leaders who are not willing to look upon change as a challenge to
adapt and grow will eventually lose effectiveness and become frustrated in
their employment. The educated security manager will have knowledge of
conventional security disciplines, other risk management disciplines, business structures, and market conditions.

In contrast, the truly successful security manager will have knowledge of
all of these things and be able to apply them to his or her own situation,
organization, and department. By applying Sun Tzu's concepts of the unconventional and conventional, normal and extraordinary, the security manager
will have infinite resources available.

Dynamics of the Conventional and Unconventional

Life is dynamic and change is inevitable. In warfare, change can mean the
difference between life and death, destruction and victory. In business, change
can make the difference between profitability and ruin. In politics, the failure
to recognize and respond to the changing political landscape can make the
difference between holding on to power and losing it. Every leader must
understand and accept the inevitability of change and learn how to make the
most of it when it comes. This ability to modify one's courses of action, business models, strategies, and thought processes is called adaptation.

Sun Tzu said, "That the army is certain to sustain the enemy's attack without suffering defeat is due to the operations of the extraordinary and the normal forces. . . . Generally, in battle, use the normal force to engage; use the extraordinary to win" (Griffith) (p. 91).

Sun Tzu continues a few lines later,

> Now the resources of those skilled in the use of extraordinary forces are as infinite as the heavens and earth; as inexhaustible as the flow of the great rivers. . . . The musical notes are only five in number but their melodies are so numerous that one cannot hear them all. The primary colors are only five in number but their combinations are so infinite that one cannot visualize them all. . . . In battle there are only the normal and extraordinary forces, but their combinations are limitless; none can comprehend them all. (Griffith) (pp. 91–92)

Here, Sun Tzu was referring to a commander's ability to win victories through a combination of both conventional and special tactics. While every commander would be expected to understand the basics of attack and defense, formation, and movement, Sun Tzu indicates that those command-ers who only know conventional forms of war will be unable to adapt to the vital changes that take place on the field of battle. When Sun Tzu states that the army typically engages the enemy through the use of normal forces or tactics, but wins through the use of special tactics or forces, he indicates the need for leaders to adapt the conventional to the situation at hand. Thus, the commander who understands both the conventional tactics of warfare and can adapt them to his particular situation will have inexhaustible resources (Figure 9-1).

Adaptation and the Security Manager

Security managers must similarly adapt to the ever-changing landscape or operational environment in which they find themselves. In today's business world, organizations are consistently asked to be more efficient, utilizing fewer resources, less money, and fewer personnel to accomplish ever-expanding organizational goals and departmental objectives.

Conventional Security Management Knowledge

Security managers must consistently adapt tactics to the new operational realities and to do so must possess a solid understanding of the conventional

Figure 9-1   *Victory is brought about by mixing the conventional and unconventional in innumerable ways.*

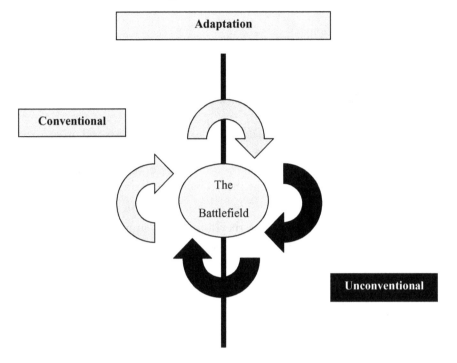

and unconventional. Though not an exhaustive list, conventional knowledge in security would include all of the following:

1. Basic management and people skills

2. Risk and vulnerability assessment

3. Countermeasure development

4. Deterrence theory

5. Detection—alarms and cameras

6. Delay—barriers and locks

7. Denial—security forces and other response capabilities

8. Emergency planning

9. Bomb threats and workplace violence

10. Investigative skills

Conventional knowledge could also include

1. Business goals

2. Business models

3. Market conditions

4. Regulatory environment

Unconventional Knowledge

If security managers have knowledge of all of the above areas and other areas that are closely related, they can be considered educated in their field. By contrast, security managers who have knowledge of all of the above areas and ones like them and can adapt that knowledge to their organization are proficient and skillful.

Adaptation and application are, therefore, keenly important. No one can really teach someone how to adapt in a formal setting, such as a classroom. This can only occur through direct experience in the field.

In order to determine whether you are adaptable to the battlefield, ask yourself the following questions:

1. Do you enjoy new challenges, or do you look upon them with dread and frustration?

2. Do you personally want to continually learn new techniques and disciplines, or are you satisfied with your current level of knowledge?

3. Are you constantly looking to better the organization and your entire department, or do you want to do the same thing day after day, year after year?

4. Do you hate the phrase, "We've never done it that way before"?

5. Do you look upon mandates to make do with fewer resources as a chance to become more efficient or as a recipe for disaster?

6. Do you view the entire organization exclusively through the prism of your work as a security manager, or can you understand business decisions that make your job more difficult?

7. Do you respect other risk management and business disciplines, or do you think they have nothing to do with your department?

8. Are the glory days behind you or ahead of you?

9. Do you come to an agreement or at least an understanding with fellow employees with whom you disagree?

10. Are you constantly angry, tired, and frustrated, or do you love your job, feel energetic and ready to go into work each day?

If you find yourself consistently looking at the negative, avoiding change and viewing the entire organization only through the eyes of a security professional and not as a manager as well, then you probably need to work on your adaptive skills or find an organization where you *can* be excited about going to work each day.

Chapter 9 Scenario 1

A pandemic has broken out and 50% percent of your entire organization's workforce, including the security department, is unavailable due to sickness, to staying home with sick relatives, or to public authorities closing off certain areas of the city to travel. What steps are you going to take to adapt to this situation?

Chapter 9 Scenario 2

As the result of a major reorganization of corporate services, your department has been assigned to take over responsibility for business continuity planning. You are expected to maintain your current security mission. No new employees will be added to your staff. All of the former business continuity employees have either left the organization or transferred to other departments. How will you adapt?

Discussion Questions

1. Why is the ability to adapt to changes important in warfare?

2. Why is the ability to adapt to changes important in the workplace?

3. Describe a situation in which you or someone you know used an unconventional technique to solve a problem?

4. Why did Sun Tzu say, "Generally, in battle, use the normal force to engage; use the extraordinary to win" (Griffith) (p. 91)? What application does that statement have for us as security managers?

5. Are you adaptable?

6. Sun Tzu said, "A military force has no constant formation. Water has no constant shape; the ability to gain victory by changing and adapting according to the opponent is called genius" (Cleary) (p. 49). What is the meaning of this statement, and how does it apply to you and your department?

7. Is it possible to teach adaptability in a classroom setting? Why or why not?

10 *Avoid Predictability*

*A military operation involves deception. Even though you are competent,
appear to be incompetent. Though effective, appear to be ineffective.*
Sun Tzu

Executive Summary

In Chapter 9, we discussed Sun Tzu's exhortation to be adaptable to the
battlefield as well as to the actions of the enemy. This chapter examines the
other side of that equation: the level of predictability with which your intent,
movement, and actions can be anticipated and adapted to. After a discussion
of the role that predictability plays in warfare, business, and politics, the
chapter ends with 30 suggestions that can make your organization less
predictable while still maintaining order.

Predictability: The Ultimate Strategic Advantage or Detriment

If you knew the course of future events and understood what steps were
within your own power to change the outcomes, you would possess an
unsurpassed strategic advantage. If your adversary possessed this knowledge,
you would be hopelessly lost—defeated before ever having a chance to
engage in battle.

Sun Tzu illustrated this point when he said,

> Appear where they cannot go, head for where they least expect you.
> To travel hundreds of miles without fatigue, go over land where there
> are no people. To unfailingly take what you attack, attack where there

is no defense. To unfailingly secure defense, defend where there is no attack. So in the case of those who are skilled in attack, their opponents do not know where to defend. In the case of those skilled in defense, their opponents do not know where to attack. (Cleary) (pp. 40–41)

In warfare, the ability to predict the enemy's movements, positions, and intentions provides a clear advantage. Armies that are easily predictable will find themselves the victim of those who are more subtle in their intentions, secretive about their positions, and stealthy in their movements.

In business, the competitor who maintains secrecy will be at a distinct advantage over the rival firm that broadcasts its new product lines before they are ready to be sold, tips its hand about pending acquisitions, and fails to protect its most sensitive data.

In politics, the party or candidate that has a predictable platform, campaign strategy, and easily identifiable weakness will surely lose. The candidate or party that is perceived to have new ideas, possesses a unique campaign strategy, and more effectively conceals weakness is far more likely to be victorious.

The same can be said in the security field. The security operations department that consistently patrols facilities according to a single pattern will eventually have that vulnerability exploited. The investigations group that always conducts travel and expense audits within certain parameters will allow a certain amount of fraud to escape its grasp. The security training and awareness function that always presents the same material in the same way will have employees lose interest and become complacent. The firm that fails to periodically conduct checks on employee activity will experience betrayal.

The Balance

The fact is that predictability equals targetability. This is true in warfare, business, politics, and the security field as well. The more predictable a person or an organization is, the more vulnerable they are to their adversaries. The apparent simplicity of the concept belies the difficulty that most people and organizations have in trying to avoid predictability while maintaining some semblance of order.

In Chapter 9, we discussed how the commander of an army or the manager of the security department must have an understanding of the conventional and unconventional, the orthodox and the unorthodox. In the context of warfare, this concept is true both when adapting your attack to the changing battlefield and when adapting your defense by avoiding predictability. Just as one could not effectively utilize only unconventional methods for attack, neither is the exclusive use of unconventional methods effective for defense.

In the security field, it once again comes down to the leadership's level of skill. Can the leader mix the conventional methods of security management with unconventional techniques designed to reduce predictability and the resulting vulnerability to the organization? The degree to which this is accomplished will determine how much of the organization's vulnerability is related to predictability and how much is related to other strategic factors.

Avoiding Predictability

When examining an organization's security and business operations, it is of critical importance to add an element of randomness into the system. The following are some suggestions on how to go about this task:

1. Ensure that patrol routes are varied and conducted at unpredictable intervals.

2. Conduct penetration studies on a regular basis to ensure that security personnel conducting access control, as well as the general employee population, remain vigilant to the possibility of unauthorized persons in the facility.

3. Conduct periodic social engineering exercises by having an outside contractor call security personnel and employees. The caller should attempt to solicit confidential information.

4. Conduct surprise audits of the security staff to ensure that they understand the postorders.

5. Conduct surprise audits of laptop computers and other information security-related items to ensure that organizational policies are being followed.

6. Conduct surprise exercises of team-level security staff relating to critical incidents such as medical emergencies.

7. If your facility scans mail and other incoming packages, insert an inert device or some other type of contraband to assess the effectiveness of the screening procedures.

8. Have an outside contractor conduct surveillance of your facility and see if anyone reports the activity to you.

9. Randomly reward employees for doing something positive to impact the security program.

10. Periodically conduct a change of posts for line-level security personnel.

11. Where possible, periodically change the shift or area of the facility in which an individual security officer works. This is done to reduce the risk that the security officer will become too close to the employees in a given area.

12. Conduct covert customer service surveys of security personnel to ensure that they are not only enforcing the rules of the organization, but that they are doing so with courtesy.

13. Audit all access systems, including cards, histories, and changes to the system on a regular basis, as well as make intermittent surprise audits.

14. Periodically come in early and/or stay late or have someone else do the same in order to observe traffic patterns and other activity.

15. Periodically review video of critical areas to observe traffic patterns or other patterns of activity.

16. Conduct periodic rechecking of employee background information.

17. Conduct periodic rechecking of business partners' and contractors' background information.

18. Develop informants within critical areas of the firm. Be sure to include service personnel, as they often are in a good position to view activity that other types of employees may miss.

19. If the situation warrants, your department is financially capable, and counsel advises you of the legality of the action, it can be effective to insert undercover investigators into critical areas of the firm or areas where significant problems have taken place. The information gleaned from quality operatives can provide the security manager with a wealth of information.

20. Review employee e-mail and Internet usage.

21. Review employee access histories.

22. Conduct regular audits of travel and expense reports.

23. Where legally advisable, utilize covert cameras to record employee activities in critical areas as well as in areas where problems have occurred in the past. This should be done in addition to overt cameras deployed around the facility.

24. If your firm uses a document destruction firm, have a security representative periodically follow the vendor to ensure that your confidential waste is actually being disposed of instead of sold.

25. Regularly review popular social networking Web sites and blogs where employees, vendors, ex-employees, or others with knowledge about the firm could post confidential company information.

26. If an employee is observed to be routinely working during hours when no one else is around, observe his actions closely.

27. Periodically change employee training and awareness programs to ensure that the target audience does not become complacent to the message.

28. Conduct surprise evacuation and shelter in-place drills to ensure that employee and security personnel know how to respond in an emergency.

29. Conduct surprise safety audits of traditional equipment and employee areas to ensure compliance.

30. Conduct surprise audits of cash handling, check processing, and other areas where negotiable instruments are located.

Notes

- Prior to conducting any type of exercise or drill, notify local authorities to avoid situations in which an actual response to a simulated situation is generated.

- Before conducting any investigative activity, check with your firm's legal department.

In literally hundreds of other areas, elements of randomness can be inserted into the system. A careful review of your own organization and operations should allow you to avoid the trap of predictability and better protect the firm.

Chapter 10 Scenario 1

Imagine you are a disgruntled ex-employee. You are upset at your perceived treatment while you were employed and decide to "get even." You don't want to hurt people and you don't want to get caught. Now, look at your own organization from that mind-set. What action would you take? What predictable patterns could you take advantage of? Now, as a security professional, how could you mitigate the vulnerabilities you identified?

Chapter 10 Scenario 2

Think of a program or capital expense that you have repeatedly requested but have thus far failed to implement or secure the funding for. Examine how you have made your previous cases to senior management. Did predictability play a role in why the program or funding was denied? Does the behavior of senior management and/or internal competitors have elements of predictability that, if addressed, in your case could make a difference?

Discussion Questions

1. Why does predictability lead to vulnerability?
2. What traps of predictability do security departments often fall into?
3. What steps can a department or individual take to avoid predictability?
4. What is the relationship between predictability and deception?
5. Were the September 11, 2001 attacks on the World Trade Center and Pentagon predictable? Why or why not?
6. Was the December 7, 1944 attack on Pearl Harbor predictable? Why or why not?
7. Was the Columbine school shooting predictable? Why or why not?
8. Think about the last security incident at your organization. Was it predictable? Did predictability play a factor?

▌▌ *Collect Intelligence*

> *Foreknowledge cannot be gotten from ghosts and spirits, cannot be had by analogy, cannot be found out by calculation. It must be obtained from people, people who know the conditions of the enemy.*
>
> Sun Tzu

Executive Summary

All individuals, businesses, and governments engage in some from of the intelligence process. This chapter discusses:

1. The importance of intelligence

2. Intelligence vs. information

3. The steps in the intelligence cycle

4. Sources of intelligence

5. Evaluation of an organization's intelligence capabilities

The Importance of Intelligence

The collection and analysis of information about the condition, intent, relationships, and activities of both adversaries and allies are essential functions of every organization. When most people think of the word "intelligence" or espionage, they typically think of fictional spies, such as Ian Fleming's James Bond or Tom Clancy's Jack Ryan. Others, perhaps with a bent for world affairs, may think of real spies that have come to the public's attention, such as John Walker, Aldrich Ames, and Jonathan Pollard.

Although intelligence may seem like an exotic field in which a very small number of select people are actively involved, the reality is that intelligence is an everyday occurrence that is engaged in by every human being and every organization. If this statement sounds far-fetched to you, ask yourself the following questions:

1. **Do you use a radar detector in your vehicle?** If so, you are engaged in signal intelligence. Your vehicle's radar detector is designed to intercept "hostile" transmissions and warn you of the presence of police. You have targeted the information you desire by purchasing the device and installing it in your vehicle. You collect the information by using the device, and you act on the information by slowing down in order to avoid a speeding ticket. In short, the radar detector provides you with actionable intelligence.

2. **Do you check the Department of State or one of the several commercial Web sites before traveling overseas?** If so, you are reading intelligence reports that are typically collected by overt means and placed into a report format for travelers.

3. **Do you use a stock broker or other financial adviser to make investment decisions?** If so, you are engaged in overt financial intelligence. You have targeted the information you desire, namely, the best stock picks. You have paid a professional to gather the information and analyze it for you so that you can take action on it.

4. **Do you ask your friends for recommendations about local restaurants?** If so, you are engaged in human intelligence. You have selected the information you seek—the quality of the restaurant or perhaps a movie, for example. You have made contact with someone who has that information. When your contact provides you with his or her analysis, you now have information you can use for making a decision.

Almost every action you take as an individual is based on the targeting, collection, and analysis of information from some outside source. Organizations also engage in intelligence on a daily basis. For example:

1. **Marketing studies:** Marketing studies are an analysis of information from an available target group of consumers. The purpose of this information and analysis is to decide whom to sell a product to, when to sell it, and how much it should cost.

2. **Request for proposals:** The RFP process is a formalized method for making purchasing decisions. The analysis involved is designed to provide the purchaser and user of the services with a clear understanding of where to best spend their resources.

3. **Compensation studies:** Human Resources departments may conduct a benchmarking analysis of compensation levels for particular types of

positions. The information is then used to make informed decisions as to salaries, thus leading to a competitive advantage over other firms in the competition for talent.

4. **Acquisition-related due diligence:** Prior to the acquisition of another company, a firm may conduct research into the financial condition of the company, the background of the principals, the dynamic risks of doing business in the company's area of operations, and several other factors. In this case, the firm wants information that will inform its decision as to whether or not to purchase the company.

Perhaps the most commonly considered organizations that engage in intelligence gathering are governments. They carry out:

1. **Military intelligence:** A country may gather and analyze information on the military capabilities of an adversary or an ally in order to make better national security decisions.

2. **Law enforcement intelligence:** A law enforcement agency may conduct research and analysis into the backgrounds of individuals and organizations with alleged ties to organized crime. The purpose of this research and analysis is to build cases for prosecution against the suspects and their organizations.

3. **Diplomatic intelligence:** A country may collect and analyze information on the foreign and domestic policies and intentions of their adversaries and allies. The purpose of this research is to make better informed political decisions.

4. **Economic intelligence:** A country may conduct research into the economic capabilities and intentions of foreign companies. The purpose of this activity is to provide information to the country's own firms so that they can be more competitive in the global economy.

Intelligence gathering is not only very common, but it influences every organization, government, and individual, even though most of us do not think of intelligence in these precise terms.

The Intelligence Cycle

As we can see in the preceding examples, intelligence denotes characteristics that go beyond simple information. Information can be on any topic and may or may not be relevant to a specific problem or the accomplishment of an objective. At the same time, intelligence is specific and applicable to real-world problems and situations. In short, information can exist independent of analysis or action; intelligence cannot.

The intelligence process that security professionals should use includes the following seven steps:

1. **Obey laws and ethical principles:** Prior to starting an intelligence program, security managers must ensure that they are being compliant not only with the minimal standards of law, but with the more stringent standards of ethical behavior and morality as well.

2. **Select target information**: Since the purpose of intelligence is to make informed and calculated decisions, the appropriate targeting of information is exceptionally important. The information targeted must be in alignment with the organization's goals and objectives, market conditions, risks, vulnerabilities, potential impacts, and potential opportunities. In other words, the needs of the organization will dictate what information should be targeted.

3. **Collect information:** After the organization has decided or targeted what information it needs, it must go about seeking that information. When collecting information there are two basic means and multiple sources. The basic means are overt (also known as open source) and covert (also known as nonpublic or confidential information).

   Some sources of overt or open source information may include

   a. Colleagues

   b. Commercial databases

   c. Web sites

   d. Professional organizations

   e. Academic papers and reports

   f. Journals

   g. Newspapers, magazines, and newsletters

   Some sources of covert or confidential information may include

   a. Colleagues

   b. Private investigators

   c. Informants

   d. Databases

   e. Internal records

   f. External records shared with the department

4. **Analyze the information:** Once information is collected through various sources and methods, it must be analyzed and interpreted. This time-consuming process is critical because it is during this phase that information begins to take on more of the characteristics of intelligence. Sources and information are rated for accuracy and are cross checked with other sources. The person conducting the analysis must be as thorough as possible, looking at all the possible meanings of the information.

5. **Report the information:** Once the information has been analyzed, it must be reported to decision makers in the most objective way possible. This is often difficult because employees generally like providing good news to their superiors, but shy away from being the harbingers of bad news.

6. **Apply the information to real-world decisions:** This is the step where mere information becomes actionable intelligence. The information has been targeted in accordance with organizational needs, collected from a variety of sources analyzed by the most objective means available, and presented to the decision makers. At this point, the management of the organization needs to make a decision and act on it.

Figure 11-1 *The intelligence cycle is a never-ending process.*

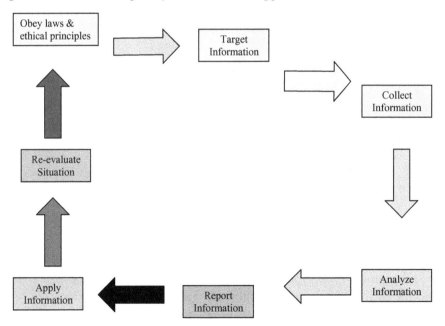

7. **Reevaluate:** Every decision has consequences, and the decisions made by management in stage 6 change the operational realities. The organization must then start the process anew to assess where it is now and what information it requires in order to move forward in its objectives and goals.

Evaluating Your Intelligence Capability

When evaluating your own organization's intelligence capability, ask yourself the following questions:

1. Have senior management, yourself, legal counsel, compliance, the ethics officer, and any other relevant parties within your organization review the scope and objectives of the program? This needs to be done before proceeding with any such program.

2. Does your organization have clear-cut goals and objectives? Without clear objectives and goals, the intelligence program will be ineffective because it will not understand what information is relevant and what information is not.

3. What types of information would help your organization meet those goals and objectives?

4. Is the information needed legally obtainable? If it is not legally obtainable, then you must reassess your information needs. Is there some other source of information that could answer the same questions?

5. What sources of information do you have available to you?

6. How accurate is your view of these sources?

7. How objective is your analysis capability?

8. Has senior management placed pressure on the analyst to come to certain conclusions? If so, the effectiveness of the program will be severely limited.

Intelligence: A Key Concept

Intelligence is a key concept in the successful conduct of war, diplomacy, business, and everyday life. The security manager who understands the need to continually gain knowledge and apply it to day-to-day operations will be better positioned to protect the organization being served. The organization that supports this effort will be more competitive in the marketplace, and the nation that successfully masters the intelligence process will maintain its national security posture even in the face of strong rivals.

As Sun Tzu noted, "So only a brilliant ruler or a wise general who can use the highly intelligent for espionage is sure of great success" (Cleary) (p. 114).

Chapter 11 Scenario

Describe in detail how you would go about setting up an intelligence program at your organization. If such a program already exists, what changes do you think could be made to improve the program?

Discussion Questions

1. What is intelligence?

2. What is the difference between intelligence and information?

3. Why is intelligence important?

4. Describe each part of the intelligence cycle.

5. Why is it important for senior management not to pressure those conducting intelligence analysis to come up with specific conclusions?

6. Do you think it is possible for an analyst to be objective?

7. Describe how individuals, organizations, and governments engage in the intelligence process every day.

12 *The Art of War and Homeland Security*

*A victorious army first wins and then seeks battle. A defeated army
first battles and then seeks victory.*

Sun Tzu

Executive Summary

The events of September 11, 2001, have resulted in monumental changes in
the security posture of the United States and its allies. This chapter discusses
some of the challenges brought about by the war on terrorism and applies
Sun Tzu's concept of strategic assessments to that conflict.

"Objectivity" and the War on Terror

Despite popular and persistent claims to the contrary, absolute objectivity is
completely outside the realm of human nature. Although a professional
should try to be dispassionate when making professional decisions, it must
be done with the acknowledgment that we are all influenced by our experience and core values. Anyone who tells you that they are completely objective is either lying or exceptionally uninformed. So, in the interest of personal
and professional integrity, let me reveal my own bias to the reader before
proceeding any further on this controversial subject.

I am a right-wing, conservative Republican who is pro-military and pro-
police and believes that societal order and security must come before the
personal liberty of any individual or interest group. These life positions
influence how I see the world. If I were a left-wing, liberal Democrat who
distrusted the police and believed that liberty gives birth to order, then this
would also influence how I see the world. Either way, I'm not objective.
Neither are you. Neither are the politicians, the military officials, the police,

the business leaders, or the security professionals. Keep this in mind when you read anything regarding the war on terror or security issues in general. Paying close attention to who your sources are and obtaining information from a wide variety of them is the only way to even come close to approaching "objectivity" on this subject.

September 11, 2001—A Watershed Event

The events of September 11, 2001, clearly illustrate that technologically advanced and interdependent societies are vulnerable to disruptive acts committed by small groups of highly committed adversaries. The attacks on the American homeland, as well as the subsequent incidents in Spain, the United Kingdom, and elsewhere, have brought terrorism to the forefront of societal discourse and public policy. The havoc created by so few people, in so short a time, has led to significant changes on both the domestic and foreign fronts.

In the five years since 9/11, we've seen several U.S. government agencies reorganized under the newly created Department of Homeland Security. The Patriot Act was passed and signed into law. The U.S. intelligence and law enforcement communities refocused their mission on terrorism and have lessened their focus on other threats such as the war on drugs. The media now routinely broadcast news items relating to security issues at airports, mass transit facilities, public venues, and large office complexes. Public discourse now commonly concentrates on the balance between civil liberties and security. Air travel, already cumbersome owing to market conditions, has become even more so due to stepped-up security procedures.

On the foreign front, American military forces have toppled the Taliban government in Afghanistan and Saddam Hussein in Iraq. Several terror plots have been foiled, and many terrorist leaders have been captured or killed. Despite these successes, terror groups continue to exist and operate on a global scale. The insurgency in Iraq continues to disrupt the implementation of a stable and strong Iraqi government, and terrorist organizations continue to threaten more attacks against the Western powers. Add to these the nuclear ambitions of terrorist-sponsoring states like Iran, and the situation becomes even more complex.

The Wrong Question

After all this change, ordinary citizens, business leaders, and government officials are still asking the same wrong question: *Are we safer now than we were five years ago?* The question is wrong on two counts:

1. The question is politically motivated.

   a. In answering this question, Republicans will point to foiled terror plots, captured and killed terrorist leaders, and disposed despots like Saddam Hussein and the Taliban, and say, "Look what a great job we've done." The implication here is that all of this action has reduced the capacity of the terrorist to wage war against the homeland. This is probably true, but is the reduction really that significant?

   b. In answering the same question, the Democrats will say, "Where is Osama Bin Laden? You've had five years to capture him! You've taken away some of our civil rights and committed our youth to an entangling foreign war." The implication here is that the capture of Osama Bin Laden would necessarily defeat al Qaeda. In reality, it would not, as professional terrorist organizations, like large companies, have succession plans.

2. The answer to the question doesn't really tell us anything of operational value.

   a. Are terrorists likely to take over aircraft and crash them into tall buildings again? Probably not; in the post–9/11 era, the passengers wouldn't allow it. So, we are safer today from a September 11-style attack than we were five years ago. Is that really of any significant help in day-to-day security planning?

   b. Has life become more difficult for terrorists? Yes, many terrorists and suspected terrorists have been captured and killed; funds have been frozen; and preemptive strikes against terrorist groups are becoming more commonplace. So, we are safer from those particular terrorists today than we were before they were captured or killed. We can even say that since their networks have been damaged, they are less capable of carrying out attacks than they were before this intervention, but, again, this doesn't really help that much in day-to-day security planning.

The Right Questions

If the wrong questions are those that are exclusively motivated by politics and lack relevance to day-to-day operations, what then are the right questions? The right questions are those that recognize the problem at hand and offer solutions in and of themselves or at least a means to a solution.

The Government

Right or more proper questions to ask about the war on terror from the standpoint of the government include the following:

1. What is the relative value of security vs. civil liberty in our society?

2. What terrorist groups most concern us and why?

3. What types of attacks are we planning for?

4. What elements of society form the most critical pieces of infrastructure?

5. Can all of these elements be defended with the resources we have at our disposal?

6. If they are not all defendable, do force multipliers exist that can be used to lessen the risk or mitigate the effects of a terrorist attack?

7. Of these elements of critical infrastructure, which is the most at risk to terrorist attack?

8. Of these elements of critical infrastructure, which is the most vulnerable to terrorist attack?

9. Of these elements of critical infrastructure, which would have the greatest potential impact on the nation if attacked?

10. Does the government have a responsibility to protect noncritical infrastructure? Why? If so, what is the level of responsibility? Which level of government?

11. Who is primarily responsible for protecting noncritical infrastructure?

12. What would be the psychological impact on the populace if noncritical infrastructure were attacked and thousands of people died? At this point, does noncritical infrastructure become critical because of the large loss of life and the accompanying political consequences?

13. With limited resources at our disposal, how do we strike a balance between the war on terrorism and the war on drugs, street crime, organized crime, public corruption, dealing with economic issues, education, and so on?

14. How can we most effectively damage the adversary's ability to attack us?

15. Is there an acceptable long-term political solution that will help us achieve our goals?

These questions and issues are just the tip of the proverbial iceberg when dealing with the challenges of homeland security from the government's perspective. Literally hundreds of questions need to be asked. Thankfully, some people in government are asking these types of questions, but one would hardly recognize this fact by looking at the current public discourse on the subject.

The Private Sector

Right or more proper questions to ask about the war on terror from the standpoint of the private sector include the following:

1. What assets are we trying to protect from terrorist attack?

2. What types of terrorist attack are we most concerned about?

3. Which terrorist organizations are we most concerned about and why?

4. What is the actual risk of a terrorist attack at a given facility?

5. What is the actual risk of a terrorist attack on a nearby facility that may affect our operations?

6. What are the vulnerabilities to terrorist attack at any given facility?

7. What are the potential impacts to the organization of a terrorist attack on a given facility?

8. Do we have the resources to secure our most valuable assets against the identified groups that we are concerned about and their tactics?

9. Are there force multipliers that could help to reduce the risk or mitigate the impacts of such an attack?

10. What security steps are organizationally acceptable?

11. Will a given countermeasure cost us more to implement than it is likely to save us?

12. What are other organizations in our industry doing?

13. What resources and assistance can you obtain from the government?

14. What resources and assistance can you obtain from vendors and consultants?

15. What resources and assistance can you offer and gain from benchmarking with other firms?

As with the preceding questions for government, these questions, too, are just a small fraction of the types of things that should be asked by every business and nonprofit organization. Some are asking these questions, but as with most issues related to risk management and security, many are choosing to ignore the questions and hope for the best. While acceptance of risk is a perfectly legitimate strategy, it should only be taken after a close examination of the risks, vulnerabilities, and potential impacts. Unfortunately, many organizations are looking at the complexity of these issues and are simply not making the effort.

The Big Question

Given the history, level of commitment, and sophistication of terrorist organizations and networks throughout the world, will the United States and its allies succeed in winning the war on terrorism?

Definitional Problems

What would winning the war on terrorism specifically mean? Would it mean the destruction of al Qaeda? If so, then the answer is yes, the United States and its allies will eventually either

1. Undermine the legitimacy of al Qaeda in the Middle East and thereby leave the organization ineffective and incapable of carrying out operations.

2. Hunt down and kill or capture enough of the group's members so that there are no leaders left to take their place, thereby destroying the organization's ability to carry out operations.

Would winning the war on terrorism mean neutralizing the *threat* posed by al Qaeda? If so, the United States and its allies could gain victory by the aforementioned means, or a third option, namely:

3. Come to a political settlement that allows both sides to claim victory. While this last strategy is not particularly appealing to most people (the author included), it could eventually take place. The old saw about not negotiating with terrorists is simply a cliché. The United States and several other nations have negotiated with terrorists in the past and will continue to do so in the future. Though distasteful and morally repugnant, it occurs because the perceived political cost of

negotiation is less than the perceived cost of losses associated with a long-term war with terrorists. The sad fact is, sometimes the terrorists win.

Would winning the war on terrorism mean the destruction of all terrorist groups worldwide? If so, then the obvious answer is no, the United States and its allies will never completely defeat terrorism. Terrorism has been around as long as human history. It is a weapon of the weak and will always be used against the powerful. Those who are engaged in this form of warfare may be referred to as guerrillas, asymmetric war fighters, insurgents, or freedom fighters, but their tactics are essentially the same. Since those tactics work, they will continue to be used.

Would winning the war on terrorism mean the defeat of those terrorist groups that threaten our own interests while ignoring those who do not threaten us? If so, then the United States and its allies may be able to accomplish this, but it is unlikely. As the most powerful group of nations on earth, the West is likely to engender resentment and anger from those with less power and fewer options. As a result, even the defeat of all the current organizations that threaten Western interests will be a short-lived victory. As long as the conditions that give rise to terror continue, so, too, will terrorism. Some will correctly argue that those conditions include poverty, welfare, economic policies, and racism, but they almost always fail to mention the most universal cause: human nature. Humans are innately competitive and combative, and given the proper circumstances, we will always resort to violence as an agent of social change. This fact is fundamental to understanding why conflict is inevitable.

Sun Tzu and the War on Terrorism

What would Sun Tzu say about the current war on terrorism? No one really knows for sure, but the methodologies given in *The Art of War* are instructive. In Chapter 1, entitled "Strategic Assessments," "Estimates," or "Initial Estimations," depending on the translation, Sun Tzu outlines the method by which one can assess who will win and who will lose a war (Cleary; Griffith; Sawyer). In Chapter 5 of the present book, we examined this process as it relates to security managers. Now we will apply it to the war on terrorism, breaking it down as Sun Tzu broke down strategic assessments into the following areas:

- **"The Way"**: Which side is superior at cultivating a sense of mission and loyalty among the populace?

While al Qaeda certainly has the ability to obtain loyal followers, their entire mission is based on the need for an outside enemy and a commitment to the spread of Islamic radicalism. The fact that they are motivated by their religious views makes it likely that the conflict will drag out for years. Their tactics, however, make it likely that they will increase their number of powerful enemies.

On the other hand, the United States, at present, has a committed leadership and a committed military, but the population seems to be influenced more and more by popular culture, trends, and mass media than it does by reasoned argument and true commitment. This could change if the United States came under significantly increasing attacks that targeted population centers and soft targets such as restaurants, schools, and shopping malls. If the United States stays engaged, attacks on population centers will eventually reoccur.

> **Advantage—U.S.:** The United States has the military power to make life very difficult for al Qaeda. As this occurs, al Qaeda will strike more U.S. targets. In doing so, it will strengthen U.S. resolve.

- **The Weather:** What external conditions will affect operations, and whom do they favor?

Al Qaeda has the advantage of surprise, being able to strike at the United States quickly and covertly. Al Qaeda also enjoys support in certain sectors of the Middle East and shares mutual enemies with other terrorist organizations who may be willing to assist in carrying out operations on al Qaeda's behalf. This advantage allows the group to drag out the conflict and hope that internal divisions will cause the United States to retreat from the world stage.

The United States has an exceptionally strong technological advantage, as well as a military and intelligence community that is second to none. With time, the United States will penetrate more and more of al Qaeda's cells and cause significant disruption to its finances and other aspects of its networks. If the United States stays the course, it is likely to nullify al Qaeda's advantage of stealth.

> **Advantage—al Qaeda:** Given the tendency of Americans to want things done yesterday, it is unlikely that the population has the patience to sustain a long-term, low-intensity conflict. It is equally unlikely that the United States can quickly defeat al Qaeda. If the U.S. population supports the war effort over time, the United States will certainly prevail. At the moment this scenario seems unlikely, unless al Qaeda makes some serious errors.

- **The Terrain:** Which side is better positioned to take advantage of the environment?

Although the United States and other Western nations are rightly making efforts to protect critical infrastructure, none of these nations has the ability to be strong at every possible point of attack; thus, al Qaeda has a potentially rich hunting ground in open societies. As Sun Tzu noted, "For if he prepares in the front his rear will be weak, and if to the rear, his front will be fragile. If he prepares to his left his right will be vulnerable and if to the right, there will be few on his left. And when he prepares everywhere he will be weak everywhere" (Griffith). As a result, al Qaeda is capable of carrying out multiple attacks in the homeland.

As previously noted, the United States has the advantage of technology and power. This advantage can be used effectively to find and destroy safehouses and other assets in offensive operations.

> **Advantage—al Qaeda:** The ability to strike at undefended targets gives the terrorists the ability to inflict physical and psychological harm while disrupting infrastructure and causing divisions among the people and political leaders.

- **Leadership:** Which side has the more capable leadership?

Unfortunately, al Qaeda's current leadership has shown an ability to carry out sophisticated operations and gain loyal followers. There is no shortage of Jihadists willing to attack the United States and even lead operations. However, given the disproportionate level of resources enjoyed by the United States, it is doubtful that al Qaeda's pool of potential leadership is significantly deep enough to offset the advantage enjoyed by the United States. The United States enjoys the resources of a professional military, a professional intelligence community, and a formal education and training system that are superior to anything al Qaeda can approach.

> **Advantage—U.S.:** The United States has a breadth and depth of leadership that stretches from line-level officers all the way to the top echelon positions. Al Qaeda has significantly fewer available resources to train and develop leaders. As a result, the United States holds a significant advantage in leadership.

- **Discipline:** Which side has a clearer system of rewards and punishments?

The operatives of al Qaeda are drawn from the dispossessed peoples of the Middle East. These operatives are motivated by their own experiences and their hatred of the United States. They possess street-smart intelligence and are fiercely loyal to the organization. The discipline required of al Qaeda operatives is the discipline of not making mistakes and striking only when the odds are in their favor.

The United States has a professional and an experienced military supported by strong technology and intelligence capability. In direct combat, the United States typically wins engagements. The discipline of the U.S. military emanates from training and a dedication to professionalism.

> **Advantage—U.S.:** Overall, the United States enjoys an advantage in possessing a greater number of disciplined forces.

A Continual War on Terrorism

In order for al Qaeda to be victorious it must

1. Not be destroyed.

2. Continue to mount periodic attacks against soft targets.

3. Cause division within Western nations via the psychological results of high casualties, spreading fear and creating the accompanying economic disruption.

4. Convince the Western populace that the war is not in their interest, thus forcing the withdrawal of Western powers from the world stage.

In order for the United States and its allies to be victorious, they must

1. Destroy al Qaeda or neutralize the threat caused by al Qaeda.

2. Prevent or significantly mitigate the most devastating attacks against the homeland.

3. Change the mindset of the American people so that they will understand and support the war on al Qaeda.

The United States and its allies will eventually defeat al Qaeda because the West has a greater number of strategic factors in its favor. Western military forces are more numerous and better supported. They have superior technology, superior training, and superior intelligence capability, as well as better overall leadership and discipline.

Defeating al Qaeda, however, will not end the war on terrorism, nor will it make the United States significantly less vulnerable to attacks on soft targets at home. Other groups will continue to exist and new groups will arise. The only long-term solution to terrorism is to undermine the reasons people turn to political violence in the first place. Given that humans have been seeking long-term solutions to poverty, hatred, racism, and other social problems since the dawn of history, it is likely that political violence will continue for the foreseeable future until workable, sustainable solutions to these critical issues can be agreed upon.

Conclusions

As security professionals, we must think about and respond to situations that are outside the scope of most people's experience. The burden of this responsibility weighs heavily upon us. However, we do possess the tools necessary to manage these responsibilities, and our mission is to use them to the best of our abilities. The concepts outlined in Sun Tzu's, *The Art of War* provide a strong framework for understanding and winning conflict in the most efficient and peaceful way possible. May you and your organization find them valuable in waging and winning your own "war."

Appendix: The Armory

Going into battle requires preparation. Just as the successful generals will ensure that their troops are well equipped with the weapons of war, so, too, should security managers ensure that both they and their staff are prepared. The following pages present an overview of the tools, tactics, and strategies contained in Chapters 1–12. These include diagrams, lists, worksheets, and charts that the security manager can use in day-to-day situations. The information in this appendix, as well as the discussion questions and scenarios at the end of each chapter, are meant to be actively used by the reader. As with the rest of this book, the information contained in the appendix was inspired by Sun Tzu's *The Art of War*. It is hoped that the reader will continue to apply the concepts illustrated in the original *Art of War*, as well as the interpretations in the current work, into day-to day operations.

Job Aid 1-1: 10 Steps to Organizational Effectiveness

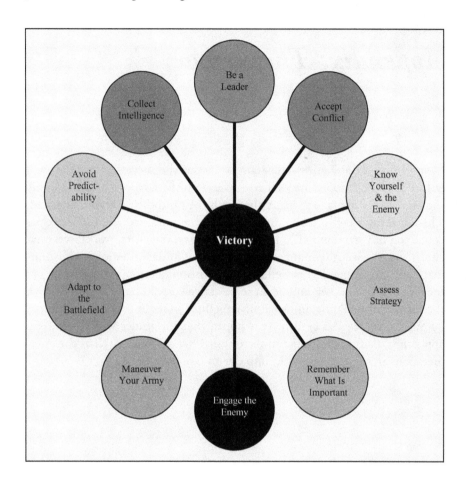

Job Aid 1-2: A Convergence of Security Threats into a True All-Hazards Environment

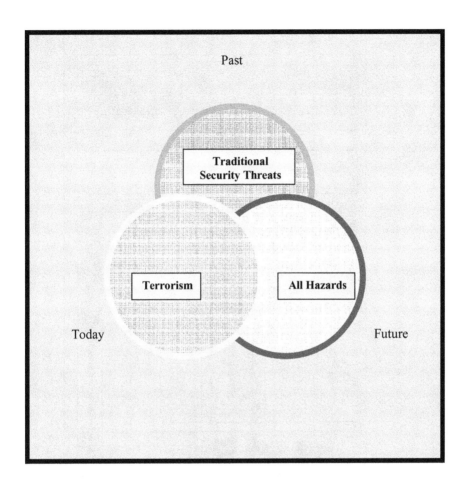

Job Aid 1-3: What Are We Up Against: 10 Most Dangerous Enemies of the Security Manager

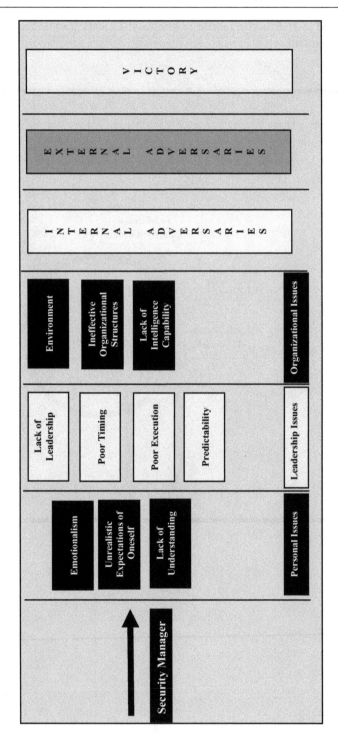

Job Aid 2-1: Five Characteristics of Successful Leaders

> - Intelligence
>   - Ability to learn
>   - Ability to reason
>   - Ability to understand the situation at hand
> - Trustworthiness
>   - Loyalty—Supports the mission, organization, and staff
>   - Consistency—Does not show favoritism
>   - Responsibility—Supports own actions and sanctioned actions of staff
>   - Integrity—Doesn't change position to suit audience
>   - Personal relationships—Performs actions that tend to transcend all arenas of life
> - Humaneness
>   - Morality—Practices a moral code that is beyond oneself
>   - Mission—Possesses a sense of purpose beyond oneself
>   - Compassion—Exhibits compassion toward others
>   - Credit—Acknowledges contributions of his or her staff
>   - Patience—Privately correct performance issues
> - Courage
>   - Calmness—Brings a sense of calm to any given situation
>   - Integrity—Understands that integrity matters
>   - Understanding—Understands human frailties
>   - Loyalty—Earns the respect of staff
>   - Vitality—Becomes vital to the organization
> - Sternness
>   - Clear expectations—Makes expectations known to the staff
>   - Evaluations—Continually evaluates own and staff's performance
>   - Confrontations—Is willing to confront people when necessary
>   - Follow-through—Acts on decisions
>   - Calculation—Calculates total value of decisions

Job Aid 2-2: Five Failures of Leadership

Recklessness—Is likely to ignore the potential for losses

Excessively cautious—Will not engage the enemy; accomplishes little

Easily angered—Allows emotions to control actions

Oversensitivity—Exhibits a form of arrogance; thinks that the
organization revolves around self

Proneness to Anxiety—Spends an inordinate amount of time worrying

Job Aid 3-1: Sources of Business World Conflict

All business conflicts emanate from one or more of these sources:

- Objectives
- Resources
- Influence
- Interpersonal

Ask yourself, what is the source of the conflict you are in now?

Job Aid 3-2: What Every Security Manager Needs to Know about Conflicts

> - Needs to accept the inevitability of conflict
> - Needs to understand that conflict is not necessarily bad
> - Needs to make a systematic study of conflict typologies and decide how they apply to the operational environment

Job Aid 4-1: External Adversaries

> Criminals
>   i. Petty
>   ii. Violent
>   iii. Professional
>   iv. Organized

> Competitors
>   i. Corporate espionage
>   ii. Foreign intelligence services

> Terrorists
>   i. Ideological/political
>   ii. Religious
>   iii. Single issue

> Activists (a partial list)
>   i. Abortion
>   ii. Animal rights
>   iii. Anti-taxes
>   iv. Environmental interests
>   v. Eschatology and doomsday cults
>   vi. Fair trade/free trade
>   vii. Gun rights
>   viii. Ideology and religious beliefs
>   ix. Organized labor and management
>   x. Race relations and separatist groups

Job Aid 4-2: Business Intelligence and Corporate Espionage Methods

Note: When investigating whether these intelligence-gathering techniques have been directed against your firm, careful consideration should be given to moral, ethical, and legal requirements. Always seek counsel from your organization's ethics officer and legal counsel in such matters.

Method	Characteristics
Open-Source Information	Legal research through the Internet, magazines, newspaper articles, public records, reports, and other freely obtainable information.
Use of Investigators	Specific techniques may include surveillance, pretext calling, record searches, interviews, and undercover operations. Can be done legally or illegally depending on the specific situation and jurisdiction.
Dumpster Diving	Obtaining information about an organization by sifting through its trash, looking for internal memos, reports, and so on. In some jurisdictions, an investigator can legally take trash that is put out on a curb for pick-up. However, if the investigator has to trespass to collect the information, the activity is considered illegal.
Undercover Operatives	The placement of undercover operatives in a competitor's organization for the purpose of obtaining confidential information is illegal. While an organization can place operatives within their own organization to investigate internal crime and violations of company policy, the organization cannot direct these efforts outside.
Listening Devices, Storage Devices, and Cameras	Use of technology to download or record confidential information about a competitor. MP3 players with large storage capacity, cellular telephones that are equipped with cameras, wireless cameras, and traditional listening devices are but a few examples.
Social Engineering	A psychosocial technique designed to obtain confidential information through misrepresentation, misdirection, and manipulation of a target. This may include pretext calling and other forms of misrepresentation designed to solicit information.
Hacking	Breaking into a firm's networks for the purpose of obtaining confidential information stored on computers. A wide variety of adversaries ranging from individuals to hacking groups, organized crime, and intelligence organizations engage in hacking.
Compromise of Employees	Soliciting information from employees of the target organization through incentives or threats. Incentives may include offers of money, jobs, gifts, or sexual favors. The target employee may also be threatened with harm to himself, his family, or public disclosure of potentially damaging private information. In some cases, ideology may be used as a basis for compromise.

Job Aid 4-3: Antiterrorism Techniques

Source: Adapted from the New York State Metropolitan Transit Authority Awareness Poster.

Technique	Explanation
Counter-Surveillance	Security personnel and employees must be watchful for people who are engaged in surveillance. Surveillance may include photographs, video, notes, drawings, or simply observation.
Social Engineering and Information Gathering	Security personnel and employees need to be wary of people trying to directly or indirectly solicit information on or demonstrating an unusual interest in building systems, security procedures, schedules, organizational structures, or similar information.
Probing	Security personnel and employees need to be wary of an adversary's attempt to find vulnerabilities in security procedures. Hostile actors may attempt to gain surreptitious entry to a facility, leave unidentified parcels in common areas to observe the response of security, or otherwise find ways to compromise the integrity of the security program.
Obtaining Equipment	Merchants, security personnel, and employees should be aware of attempts to obtain explosives, weapons, or other material that may be utilized to carry out a terrorist incident.
Awareness	The organization that focuses on security personnel and employee awareness will more likely than not "fail" a terrorist organization's target selection criteria. Although these steps may not prevent a terrorist attack from occurring, it may deflect or delay the attack to another facility, or increase the chance of intervention by law enforcement agencies.

Job Aid 4-4: Internal Adversaries

1. Personnel issues (employees or contractors)
   a. Lax attitudes
      i. "It can't happen here"
      ii. Security is an "inconvenience"
      iii. Perfunctory compliance with policies
      iv. Awareness without concern
   b. Employee theft or unauthorized use of
      i. Equipment
      ii. Money
      iii. Time
      iv. Information
      v. Personal enrichment
   c. Harassment
      i. Sexual
      ii. Race-based
   d. Internal crime
      i. Insider trading
      ii. Fraud
      iii. Drugs
   e. Workplace violence
2. Internal competitors
   a. Other departments
      i. Resources
      ii. Power/influence

Job Aid 5-1: Which Organization Has The Way?

The Way is the overall character, sense of mission, or urgency with which an organization inculcates its employees. When assessing which side has The Way, consider the following:

Fundamental Mission	**What is the mission of the organization?** ■ Does a sense of mission pervade the organization? ■ Is the organization simply a vehicle to make money? ■ Does a sense of urgency exist in everything that is done for customers whether internal or external?
Articulation and Demonstration of the Fundamental Mission	**What is the Commitment of Management?** ■ Does senior management articulate the mission? ■ Does senior management continually demonstrate the organization's mission?
People	**What type of people work for the organization?** ■ Do employees seem committed, or are they biding their time until the next opportunity presents itself? ■ Are ethical processes valued, or are they sacrificed in the name of short-term results? ■ Are employees continuing to learn and grow, or are they complacent?
Reputation	**What is the public reputation of the organization?** ■ What type of media coverage have the organization and its principals received over a long period of time? ■ How often has the organization been sued or subjected to regulatory fines? ■ What are the tone and content of the organization's public statements?
Organizational Myths	**What corporate myths exist about the organization?** ■ Is a common theme or set of themes present? If so, what do they say about the organization's culture? ■ Are the themes of these corporate legends aligned with the mission statements and actions of management?

Job Aid 5-2: The Weather

Weather refers to external conditions that influence the behavior of our own group and/or that of our adversaries. When assessing the weather, consider the following:

Market Conditions	■ Are market conditions equally distributed across the industry or firm? In other words, is the field of play equally difficult for both sides? ■ What resources does each side possess? ■ Is each side able to utilize its given resources equally? ■ Which side has the most successful experience in dealing with similar market conditions?
Regulatory Climate	■ Does the regulatory environment affect both sides equally? ■ Which side has the most experience in effectively managing these issues? ■ Which side has the requisite resources already in place? ■ Which side is in a better overall position to respond to the mandate?
Public Relations Issues	■ Which side has the clearer message? ■ Which side has a more positive reputation? ■ Which side has the most access to the media in question? ■ Which side has had the most success dealing with these issues in the past?
External Political, Religious, and Other Controversial Issues	■ Is the issue in question of importance to the organization? ■ Does the organization have a position on the issue? ■ Do management and employees support the firm's position? ■ Are plans in place to advance the firm's position? ■ Is management willing to make the "right" enemies to advance its position?

Job Aid 5-3: The Terrain

Terrain refers to the environment or field of battle in which security managers find themselves. When assessing the terrain, consider the following:

Operational Environment	▪ Which side has a more clearly defined mission?
	▪ Which side has the most support of its constituent organization?
	▪ Which side has an organizational structure that is more conducive to accomplishing its mission?
	▪ Which side has the requisite resources to carry out the mission?
	▪ Which side has superior tactics, policies, and procedures in place?
Organizational Risk Tolerance	▪ Which side has conducted a comprehensive assessment of its assets, potential loss events and impacts, threats, risks, and vulnerabilities?
	▪ Which side has implemented reasonable countermeasures to mitigate its risks?
	▪ Which side has the most to gain from taking risks?
	▪ Which side has the most to lose from taking risks?
	▪ Which side's culture values risk taking more?
Historical and Cultural Factors	▪ What previous patterns of behavior are suggested by each organization's history?
	▪ What cultural norms and mores are present for each side?

Job Aid 5-4: Leadership

Leadership is a key element in the success of an organization. When assessing an organization's leadership, consider the following:

Experience	The side that has the most experienced leadership will, by definition, have a greater reservoir of applied knowledge, including previous mistakes and successes.
Expertise	The side that has the expertise that is most relevant to the situation at hand has a distinct advantage.
Authority	The side with the superior leadership is the one whose leaders use their authority for the greater good of the organization.
Charisma	The side whose leaders have the greater ability to motivate the troops are at an advantage.
Weaknesses	Leaders are human beings and, as such, are vulnerable to human weaknesses. Impetuous leaders make unnecessarily bold moves that can endanger the group. Fearful leaders can be too cautious and miss opportunities. Leaders prone to anger can allow the adversary and internal situations to color their judgment. Leaders who seek personal glory are likely to forget the mission. Arrogant leaders are unlikely to admit vulnerabilities.

Job Aid 5-5: Discipline

Discipline is a key element in the success of an organization. When assessing an organization's discipline, consider the following:

Clear Chains of Command	■ Which side has the simplest chain of command? ■ Which side's chain of command allows for the easiest communication pathway?
Clearly Defined Processes	■ Which side's processes are easiest to understand? ■ Which side's processes are more consistent? ■ Which side's processes yield the highest quality in the shortest period of time?
Clearly Defined and Consistently Enforced Rules	■ Are the rules simple to understand? ■ Are the rules communicated to all members of the organization? ■ Are the rules consistently enforced regardless of personal relationship or position?
Clear Criteria for Rewarding Performance	■ Are the basic compensation levels within industry norms? ■ Are the basic compensation levels sufficient for an employee to make a reasonable living? ■ Are the basic expectations of all employees clearly defined and communicated? ■ Are the rewards for employees that go beyond expectations considered desirable by the widest possible base of employees? ■ Are rewards for going above expectations given out solely according to merit?
Clear Criteria for Dealing with Problems	■ Are all employees treated equally and consistently? ■ Do the procedures for dealing with discipline issues focus on the behavior in question? ■ Do the procedures allow for the development and execution of performance improvement plans?

Job Aid 5-6: Strategic Assessment Worksheet

CRITERIA	COMMENTS	ADVANTAGE
Mission What is your mission? What is your adversary's mission?		
Organization How is your adversary organized? What is the history of the adversary? What is the style of leadership?		
Allies Who are your adversary's allies? Who are your adversary's potential allies? What is your relationship with these allies and potential allies?		
Potential Areas of Conflict What is the scope of potential conflict? Are your allies in some other sphere? Is there a way of retreating from an unimportant front in order to accomplish your objective, while still giving something to the adversary? Can the adversary be turned into an ally?		
Resources What resources does your adversary have? What resources do you have?		

Job Aid 6-1: Issues of Importance to All Organizations

Money	▪ The fundamental purpose of every business is to generate revenue for the shareholders. This statement is true whether one is speaking of a small diner or a large multinational conglomerate. Even nonprofit organizations must generate revenue in the form of donations to stay solvent.
New Business Opportunities	▪ Successful organizations are quick to seize opportunities. It is the responsibility of the security manager and other risk management professionals to design protections around the business, and not vice versa.
Reputation	▪ The democratization of the media has exponentially increased the power of individuals to influence consumer behavior. The successful security manager must possess some knowledge of how the media can effect the reputation of the organization.
Vital Processes	▪ A vital process is one that must be accomplished in order for the organization to continue to exist. Typically, a vital business process has either very low or zero periods of acceptable downtime. The successful security manager must have an understanding of the vital processes so that adequate protection measures can be designed and executed. The security manager need not be an expert on all of the vital processes, but should go to great lengths to work with business lines and other support functions.
Regulatory Environment	▪ Since failure to comply with regulations can result in fines, damage to the organization's reputation and in some cases day-to-day operations, it is incumbent the organization must keep abreast of the regulatory environment and, at a minimum, maintain compliance.

Job Aid: 6-2: What Is Important to Your Organization?

When assessing what is really important to your organization, consider the following questions:

1. What are the purpose, goals, and/or mission of the organization?

2. What reputational risks does your organization face?

3. What new business opportunities are most likely to serve the organization's purposes?

4. What vital processes need to occur in order to accomplish the organization's purposes?

5. What regulatory issues are likely to affect your firm?

Job Aid 6-3: What Is Really Important to Your Department?

When assessing what is really important to your department, consider the following:

Support of Organizational Goals	■ Do the day-to-day and long-range goals of the security department directly support the goals of the organization? ■ Is there confusion between the goals of the department and the means of accomplishing the goals?
Security as a Business Partner	■ How does the security department support the acquisition of new business opportunities?
Reputation	■ How does the security department protect the image and reputation of the organization?
Protection of Vital Interests and Assets	■ How does the security department contribute to the protection of the vital business of the organization?
Regulatory Environment	■ How does the security department assist in maintaining the organization's compliance with regulatory requirements?

Job Aid 6-4: What Is Really Important to the Security Manager?

When assessing what is really important to you, consider the following:

Do you believe in the organization's mission?	■ Are you proud of the organization you work for, or is it just a job? ■ Are you biding your time until something better comes along? ■ If, despite your best efforts, you can't bring yourself to support the organization's mission, it may be time to look at employment in another organization where you are more committed.
Do you see yourself as a business manager as well as a security manager?	■ The days of just being a security manager are long gone. Today's security professionals need to have knowledge not only of security, but of business, information technology, safety, business continuity, training, and regulatory requirements. ■ The more broad-based security managers can be, while still maintaining an area of expertise, the more successful and happy they will be.
How important is the organization's and your own reputation?	■ Do you consider the organization you work for to be ethical? ■ Do you have the power to change those aspects of the organization that are ethically wrong or questionable? ■ Consider what is more important to you; your job or your career, your current financial status or your personal integrity.
Do you want to try new things, or are you content with the way things are?	■ The security manager who can change with the organizational and market conditions will be successful and content. Those who cannot will be unhappy and frustrated. Remember, we spend more time at work than anywhere else. You owe it to yourself and your family to be joyful and content.
How do you view compliance and regulatory issues?	■ If you view compliance with laws, regulations, and standards as tedious and unimportant, then so will your staff. If your staff doesn't view these issues as important, then that part of your department's mission will fail.

Job Aid 6-5: What Is Really NOT Important!

1. Doing what you've always done because it's what you've always done. The security industry and the threats we face are rapidly evolving. Those who are not willing to adapt will be unable to carry out their duties.

2. Taking on new and exciting projects simply because they are new and exciting. All projects and programs should specifically support departmental goals, which in turn support the goals of the organization. Instead of taking on a project because it is new and exciting, try making the projects you already have exciting.

3. Getting caught up in exciting projects and forgetting about core missions. Even if a new project does support the overall goals of the department and organization, it needs to be placed in perspective. Core missions should be clearly understood and prioritized accordingly.

4. Your personal glory. It's not about you! It's about the organization, the department, your staff, your coworkers, your customers, your colleagues, and your country. If you focus on doing your best, all else will follow.

Job Aid 7-1: Rank of Militarists

Rank	Risks	Values	Strategy	Victory
Grandmaster	Exceptionally Low	■ Perfection of his discipline ■ Efficiency ■ Service and leadership ■ Information and analytics	■ Wins without fighting ■ Strikes while plans are being developed ■ Breaks up alliances ■ Adversary doesn't know who foiled his plans	Always achieves victory
Master	Very Low	■ Professionalism ■ Efficiency ■ Service and leadership ■ Information and analytics	■ Wins with little or no fighting ■ Strikes in early stages of plans ■ Breaks up alliances ■ Adversary may not know who foiled his plans	Almost always achieves victory
Black Belt	Low	■ Fighting skill ■ Efficiency ■ Service and leadership	■ Wins by defeating the enemy in combat ■ Strikes weak points ■ Makes efficient use of physical techniques	Achieves victory more often than not
Red Belt	Medium	■ Fighting skill ■ Complex techniques ■ Position	■ Wins by defeating enemy in combat ■ Strikes at weak points ■ Makes fairly efficient use of physical techniques	Achieves victory about half of the time
Blue Belt	Medium/High	■ Fighting skill ■ Toughness ■ Complex techniques ■ Position	■ Wins by defeating enemy in combat ■ Strikes at weak points ■ Makes reasonably efficient use of physical techniques	Achieves victory a little less than half of the time
Green Belt	High	■ Fighting skill ■ Toughness ■ Image and position	■ Wins by defeating enemy in combat ■ Strikes wherever he can ■ Makes inefficient use of physical techniques	Seldom achieves victory
Yellow Belt	Very High	■ Fighting skill	■ Wins by defeating enemy in combat	Very seldom achieves victory

Job Aid 7-2: Invincibility vs. Vulnerability

Assumption: The rules of strategy can be known and applied.

Invincibility	Vulnerability
A leader who understands and consistently applies the rules of strategy	A leader who does not understand or consistently applies the rules of strategy
A leader can make his or her organization invincible by consistently attending to the rules of strategy	A leader leaves his or her organization vulnerable by failing to follow the rules of strategy

> "In ancient times skillful warriors first made themselves invincible, and then watched for vulnerability in their opponents. Invincibility is in oneself, vulnerability is in the opponent. Therefore skillful warriors are able to be invincible, but they cannot cause their opponents to be vulnerable. That is why it is said that victory can be discerned but not manufactured." (Cleary) (p. 25)

Job Aid 7-3: Basic Battle Strategies

Attack Advantages	Defense Advantages
The strategy of attack is for times when resources are in surplus. The reason for this is that it takes significantly more energy to mount an attack than it does to mount a defense. The objective of the attacker is to render the defender's forces useless by convincing them to surrender, trapping them, critically damaging them, or destroying them in battle.	Defense is the strategy employed by those whose forces are smaller and resources less abundant. Defense is a matter of invincibility—in other words, the objective of the defender is simply to not be defeated.
The attacker has more resources and troop strength available than does the defender.	The defender can retreat as long as he or she has an escape route. In contrast, the attacker must directly engage and defeat the defender in order to achieve victory.
The attacker typically initiates the action and thus has the element of surprise on his side. The defender must react to the attack.	The defender can avoid the attacker and still meet his or her objective. The attacker must find the defender, which takes energy and can spread his or her forces into smaller sizes whose component parts may themselves come under attack.
The attacker can operate in the open and move directly. The defender must hide and use circuitous routes of travel.	The defender can split his or her forces and make it even more difficult for the attacker to find the defender.
The attacker can cut off access to strategic areas by virtue of his superior resources.	The defender can engage in harassment of the attacker by striking weak areas and then retreating. When this happens repeatedly, the morale of the attacker suffers while the morale of the defender increases.
The attacker can sustain more damage and still emerge victorious due to superior resources and strength.	The defender can gather human intelligence more easily than can the attacker because the relative size of the attacker creates more opportunities for leaks. By contrast, the attacker must first find the smaller force of the defender and then start to gather information.

Job Aid 7-4: Choosing a Basic Battle Strategy

When assessing what basic battle strategy to employ, the leader must ask the following questions:

1. What is my objective? Do I need to conquer, or is the objective simply to keep from being defeated?

2. What is my strength compared to that of my adversary?

3. What resources do I have at my disposal?

These three questions will give the leader a basic strategy. The application of the strategy will require an understanding of force and the use of both orthodox and unorthodox tactics.

Job Aid 7-5: Engaging the Enemy in Battle

When deciding to engage in battle, the security professional should be aware of the following elements:

Preparation	▪ Have you established yourself as a leader?
	▪ Do you understand that conflict is inevitable?
	▪ Do you know yourself, your organization's capabilities, and the capabilities of your adversary?
	▪ Have you conducted a comparative strategic assessment?
	▪ Do you understand that victory and not persistence is important?
Skill	▪ How skilled are you?
Strategy	▪ What is your objective?
	▪ How does your objective drive your battle strategy?
	▪ Do you have surplus or insufficient resources?
Invincibility	▪ Do you understand and consistently follow the rules of strategy?
Vulnerability	▪ Do your opponent's vulnerabilities outweigh your own?
Force	▪ Do you apply your strength against the adversary's weakness?

Job Aid 8-1: Types of Terrain

Sun Tzu's *Art of War* describes six types of terrain that the general or, in our case, the security manager must understand in order to maneuver his army or department. The types of terrain are as follows:

Easily passable terrain	▪ This terrain is easy to move through and by itself offers no particular advantage to either side. By taking the initiative and seizing the best position first, you can gain a positional advantage.
Hung-up terrain	▪ This type of terrain is characterized by the difficulty of getting back to your original position if things do not turn out as expected. If security managers attempt a specific course of action, they must have contingencies. If they do not have contingencies in place and the plan fails badly, security managers will make their superiors question the course of action, the manager's competency, and in some cases, the mission itself.
Standoff terrain	▪ Standoff terrain occurs when it is in neither side's interest to venture forth. Typically, this occurs when a regulatory requirement or corporate policy mandates the presence of a certain program but fails to address the quality of the program as expressed in specific measurements. An adversary of the program will be compelled to participate but will do so in a nominal manner. As a result, nothing really gets accomplished.
Narrow terrain	▪ Narrow terrain can occur in a mountain pass or other areas where there is little room for maneuverability. Narrow terrain can take the form of corporate traditions that may have potentially negative security consequences. These traditions may be so well entrenched that a direct attack will cost you more than is likely to be gained. If you commit to this course of action, you may be able to retreat from it, but not without significant cost.
Steep terrain	▪ Steep terrain, like narrow terrain and hung-up terrain, offers clear advantages to the side that arrives first. When a new issue that has security implications presents itself, the security department must act immediately. Failure to do so may result in another group creating a solution that is unworkable from a security perspective.
Wide-open Terrain	▪ Wide-open terrain creates a situation in which both sides are completely exposed. Security managers who find themselves on wide-open terrain should not try to mount an attack but should instead maneuver their department into a better position. This may be accomplished by attempting to reframe the issue, waiting for the adversary to make a mistake, or withdrawing into familiar and advantageous territory.

Job Aid 8-2: Rules for Maneuvering Armies

Sun Tzu created a number of rules for the maneuverability of armies, shown here as interpreted by Cleary (in quotes). Some of those rules include:

"When fighting on a hill do not climb." (p. 67)	■ Why make your mission more difficult by trying to advance uphill onto fortified positions? Successful security managers will seek to accomplish their mission by utilizing energy efficiently.
"When cut off from the water do not meet them in the water, always stay away from the water; it is advantageous to let half of them cross and then attack them." (pp. 67–68)	■ Security managers need to avoid the traps of underestimating their adversaries and becoming complacent.
"Go right through salt marshes, just go quickly and do not tarry." (p. 68)	■ Security managers must ensure that exposures are limited.
"Take up position where it is easy to maneuver." (p. 68)	■ Security managers must ensure that they have several options open, whether dealing with an operational security threat or an internal competitor.
"Those who come seeking peace without a treaty are plotting." (p. 73)	■ Leaders must constantly compare the stated aims of their adversaries with their actions. In cases where the stated aims differ from actions, the leader needs to be extravigilant.
"If half of their force advances and half retreats, they are trying to lure you." (p. 74)	■ Security managers must observe their adversary's actions in order to ascertain whether they make sense given the circumstance. Assuming the adversary is a rational actor, this observation will inform the security manager's decisions.
"When they see an advantage but do not advance on it, they are weary." (p. 74)	■ An adversary who fails to follow up on your mistakes is either inept or tired. If you judge them to be tried, it is time to attack.

Job Aid 8-3: Moving Your Army

When assessing the direction in which to maneuver your department, the following questions should be asked.

1. What type of terrain am I on? In other words, what is your department's operational environment?

2. Which side does the terrain favor? Are you in a favorable position?

3. Should I wait for the adversary to move first? Is your best advantage to wait and see what move your competitor/opponent makes first?

4. Is my movement impeded? Are there factors that keep your department from acting?

5. Can I take circuitous routes to confuse the enemy? Is there an indirect path to achieve your department's objectives?

6. Can I take advantage of the natural features of the terrain? What is it about your organization's environment that favors your department?

7. Does withdrawing place me in a better position? Can you yield on a specific point now, in order to advance your overall objective?

8. Can I induce the adversary to come to me? How can you lure your competitor or opponent into making a careless error?

9. Can I tire the adversary by creating the appearance of movement? Is your security department being proactive in its deployment of personnel and its use of resources?

10. Can I entice the enemy to split its forces? Do the strategies and tactics of your security department cause your adversary to divide its resources?

Job Aid 9-1: Adaption

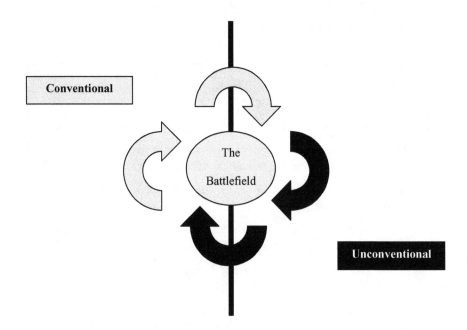

Job Aid 9-2: Conventional Security Management Knowledge

Though not an exhaustive list, conventional knowledge in security would include all of the following:

1. Basic management and people skills

2. Risk and vulnerability assessment

3. Countermeasure development

4. Deterrence theory

5. Detection—alarms and cameras

6. Delay—barriers and locks

7. Denial—security forces and other response capabilities

8. Emergency planning

9. Bomb threats and workplace violence

10. Investigative skills

Conventional knowledge could also include

1. Business goals

2. Business models

3. Market conditions

4. Regulatory environment

Job Aid 9-3: Are You Adaptable?

In order to determine whether you are adaptable to the battlefield, ask yourself the following questions:

1. Do you enjoy new challenges, or do you look upon them with dread and frustration?

2. Do you personally want to continually learn new techniques and disciplines, or are you satisfied with your current level of knowledge?

3. Are you constantly looking to better the organization and your entire department, or do you want to do the same thing day after day, year after year?

4. Do you hate the phrase, "We've never done it that way before"?

5. Do you look upon mandates to make do with fewer resources as a chance to become more efficient or as a recipe for disaster?

6. Do you view the entire organization exclusively through the prism of your work as a security manager, or can you understand business decisions that make your job more difficult?

7. Do you respect other risk management and business disciplines, or do you think they have nothing to do with your department?

8. Are the glory days behind you or ahead of you?

9. Do you come to an agreement or at least an understanding with fellow employees with whom you disagree?

10. Are you constantly angry, tired, and frustrated, or do you love your job, feel energetic and ready to go into work each day?

If you find yourself consistently looking at the negative, avoiding change, and viewing the entire organization only through the eyes of a security professional and not as a manager as well, then you probably need to work on your adaptive skills or find an organization where you can be excited about going to work each day.

Job Aid 10-1: Avoiding Predictability

1. Ensure that patrol routes are varied and conducted at unpredictable intervals.

2. Conduct penetration studies on a regular basis to ensure that security personnel conducting access control, as well as the general employee population, remain vigilant to the possibility of unauthorized persons in the facility.

3. Conduct periodic social engineering exercises by having an outside contractor call security personnel and employees. The caller should attempt to solicit confidential information.

4. Conduct surprise audits of the security staff to ensure that they understand the post orders.

5. Conduct surprise audits of laptop computers and other information security-related items to ensure that organizational policies are being followed.

6. Conduct surprise exercises of team-level security staff relating to critical incidents such as medical emergencies.

7. If your facility scans mail and other incoming packages, insert an inert device or some other type of contraband to assess the effectiveness of the screening procedures.

8. Have an outside contractor conduct surveillance of your facility and see if anyone reports the activity to you.

9. Randomly reward employees for doing something positive to impact the security program.

10. Periodically conduct a change of posts for line-level security personnel.

11. Where possible, periodically change the shift or area of the facility in which an individual security officer works in. This is done to reduce the risk that the security officer will become too close to the employees in a given area.

12. Conduct covert customer service surveys of security personnel to ensure that they are not only enforcing the rules of the organization, but that they are doing so with courtesy.

13. Audit all access systems, including cards, histories, and changes to the system on a regular basis, as well as make intermittent surprise audits.

14. Periodically come in early/stay late or have someone else do the same in order to observe traffic patterns and other activity.

(continued)

15. Periodically review video of critical areas to observe traffic patterns or other patterns of activity.

16. Conduct periodic rechecking of employee background information.

17. Conduct periodic rechecking of business partners and contractors' background information.

18. Develop informants within critical areas of the firm. Be sure to include service personnel, as they often are in a good position to view activity that other types of employees may miss.

19. If the situation warrants, your department is financially capable, and counsel advises you of the legality of the action, it can be effective to insert undercover investigators into critical areas of the firm or areas where significant problems have taken place. The information gleaned from quality operatives can provide the security manager with a wealth of information.

20. Review employee e-mail and Internet usage.

21. Review employee access histories.

22. Conduct regular audits of travel and expense reports.

23. Where legally advisable, utilize covert cameras to record employee activities in critical areas as well as areas where problems have occurred in the past. This should be done in addition to overt cameras deployed around the facility.

24. If your firm uses a document destruction firm, have a security representative periodically follow the vendor to ensure that your confidential waste is actually being disposed of instead of sold.

25. Regularly review popular social networking Web sites and blogs where employees, vendors, ex-employees, or others with knowledge about the firm could post confidential company information.

26. If an employee is observed to be routinely working during hours when no one else is around, observe his actions closely.

27. Periodically change employee training and awareness programs to ensure that the target audience does not become complacent to the message.

28. Conduct surprise evacuation and shelter in place drills to ensure that employee and security personnel know how to respond in an emergency.

29. Conduct surprise safety audits of traditional equipment and employee areas to ensure compliance.

30. Conduct surprise audits of cash handling, check processing, and other areas where negotiable instruments are located.

Job Aid 11-1: Personal Intelligence

The word "intelligence" is often thought of as an exotic art practiced only by an elite few who work for super-secret government agencies, but in reality, ordinary people use a form of intelligence every day. Here are some examples:

1. Do you use a radar detector in your vehicle? If so, you are engaged in signal intelligence.

2. Do you check the Department of State or one of the several commercial Web sites before traveling overseas? If so, you are reading intelligence reports that are typically collected by overt means and placed into a report format for travelers.

3. Do you use a stock broker or other financial adviser to make investment decisions? If so, you are engaged in overt financial intelligence. You have targeted the information you desire, namely, the best stock picks. You have paid a professional to gather the information and analyze it for you so that you can take action on it.

4. Do you ask your friends for recommendations about local restaurants? If so, you are engaged in human intelligence. You have selected the information you seek—the quality of the restaurant or perhaps a movie, for example. You have made contact with someone who has that information. When your contact provides you with his or her analysis, you now have information you can use for making a decision.

Almost every action you take as an individual is based on the targeting, collection, and analysis of information from some outside source.

Job Aid 11-2: Organizational Intelligence in the Private Sector

Intelligence is also used in the private sector. Here are just a few examples:

1. **Marketing studies:** Marketing studies are an analysis of information from an available target group of consumers. The purpose of this information and analysis is to decide whom to sell a product to, when to sell it, and how much it should cost.

2. **Request for proposals:** The RFP process is a formalized method for making purchasing decisions. The analysis involved is designed to provide the purchaser and user of the services with a clear understanding of where to best spend their resources.

3. **Compensation studies:** Human Resources departments may conduct a benchmarking analysis of compensation levels for particular types of positions. The information is then used to make informed decisions as to salaries, thus leading to a competitive advantage over other firms in the competition for talent.

4. **Acquisition-related due diligence:** Prior to the acquisition of another company, a firm may conduct research into the financial condition of the company, the background of the principals, the dynamic risks of doing business in the company's area of operations, and several other factors. In this case, the firm wants information that will inform its decision as to whether to purchase the company.

Job Aid 11-3: Intelligence in the Public Sector

Intelligence is used extensively by government agencies. Here are just a few examples:

1. **Military intelligence:** A country may gather and analyze information on the military capabilities of an adversary or an ally in order to make better national security decisions.

2. **Law enforcement intelligence:** A law enforcement agency may conduct research and analysis into the backgrounds of individuals and organizations with alleged ties to organized crime. The purpose of this research and analysis is to build cases for prosecution against the suspects and their organizations.

3. **Diplomatic intelligence:** A country may collect and analyze information on the foreign and domestic policies and intentions of their adversaries and allies. The purpose of this research is to make better informed political decisions.

4. **Economic intelligence:** A country may conduct research into the economic capabilities and intentions of foreign companies. The purpose of this activity is to provide information to the country's own firms so that they can be more competitive in the global economy.

Intelligence gathering is not only very common, but it influences every organization, government, and individual, even though most of us do not think of intelligence in these precise terms.

Job Aid 12-1: What the Government Should Be Asking about the War on Terror

1. What is the relative value of security vs. civil liberty in our society?

2. What terrorist groups most concern us and why?

3. What types of attacks are we planning for?

4. What elements of society form the most critical pieces of infrastructure?

5. Can all of these elements be defended with the resources we have at our disposal?

6. If they are not all defendable, do force multipliers exist that can be used to lessen the risk or mitigate the effects of a terrorist attack?

7. Of these elements of critical infrastructure, which is the most at risk to terrorist attack?

8. Of these elements of critical infrastructure, which is the most vulnerable to terrorist attack?

9. Of these elements of critical infrastructure, which would have the greatest potential impact on the nation if attacked?

10. Does the government have a responsibility to protect noncritical infrastructure? Why? If so, what is the level of responsibility? Which level of government?

11. Who is primarily responsible for protecting noncritical infrastructure?

12. What would be the psychological impact on the populace if noncritical infrastructure were attacked and thousands of people died? At this point, does noncritical infrastructure become critical because of the large loss of life and the accompanying political consequences?

13. With limited resources at our disposal, how do we strike a balance between the war on terrorism and the war on drugs, street crime, organized crime, public corruption, dealing with economic issues, education, and so on?

14. How can we most effectively damage the adversary's ability to attack us?

15. Is there an acceptable long-term political solution that will help us achieve our goals?

These questions and issues are just the tip of the proverbial iceberg when dealing with the challenges of homeland security from the government's perspective. Literally hundreds of questions need to be asked. Thankfully, some people in government are asking these types of questions, but one would hardly recognize this fact by looking at the current public discourse on the subject.

Job Aid 12-2: What the Private Sector Should Be Asking about the War on Terror

1. What assets are we trying to protect from terrorist attack?

2. What types of terrorist attack are we most concerned about?

3. Which terrorist organizations are we most concerned about and why?

4. What is the actual risk of a terrorist attack at a given facility?

5. What is the actual risk of a terrorist attack on a nearby facility that may affect our operations?

6. What are the vulnerabilities to terrorist attack at any given facility?

7. What are the potential impacts to the organization of a terrorist attack on a given facility?

8. Do we have the resources to secure our most valuable assets against the identified groups that we are concerned about and their tactics?

9. Are there force multipliers that could help to reduce the risk or mitigate the impacts of such an attack?

10. What security steps are organizationally acceptable?

11. Will a given countermeasure cost us more to implement than it is likely to save us?

12. What are other organizations in our industry doing?

13. What resources and assistance can you obtain from the government?

14. What resources and assistance can you obtain from vendors and consultants?

15. What resources and assistance can you offer and gain from benchmarking with other firms?

These questions are just a small fraction of the types of things that should be asked by every business and nonprofit organization. Some are asking these questions, but as with most issues related to risk management and security, many are choosing to ignore the questions and hope for the best. While acceptance of risk is a perfectly legitimate strategy, it should only be taken after a close examination of the risks, vulnerabilities, and potential impacts. Unfortunately, many organizations are looking at the complexity of these issues and are simply not making the effort.

Job Aid 12-3: What the Individual Should Be Asking about the War on Terror

1. Do I have adequate emergency supplies stockpiled in my home?

2. Do I have adequate emergency supplies stockpiled in my vehicle?

3. Is my family prepared to deal with an order to shelter in place if ordered by the authorities?

4. If my family were to become separated, do we have a designated place to meet?

5. Does each member of my family have a means to communicate in the event they become separated?

6. Has my family become more observant of people's behavior in public places?

7. Do the schools in my community have emergency plans in place?

8. Are the local first responders in my community adequately prepared to deal with a terrorist attack?

9. Do the first responders in my community regularly conduct joint exercises to keep their skills sharp?

10. Does my community have a Community Emergency Response Team (CERT) team in place?

11. What nongovernmental emergency response groups are available in my community?

12. Has my family been trained in first aid and CPR?

13. Does my neighborhood have a watch program in place?

14. Is my local police department active in the community?

15. Have risk assessments been conducted for critical infrastructure locations in my community?

As with questions for government and the private sector, these are just a few issues that should be of concern to individuals.

Job Aid 12-4: Definitional Problems of "Winning" the War on Terror

What would winning the war on terrorism specifically mean?

1. The destruction of al Qaeda?

2. The neutralizing of the *threat* posed by al Qaeda?

3. The destruction of all terrorist groups worldwide?

4. The defeat of those terrorist groups that threaten our own interests, while ignoring those who do not threaten us?

Job Aid 12-5: Sun Tzu and the War or Terror

Strategic Factors	Comments	USA	Al Qaeda
The Way	**Which side is superior at cultivating a sense of mission and loyalty among the populace?** The United States has the military power to make life very difficult for al Qaeda. As this occurs, al Qaeda will strike more U.S. targets. In doing so, it will strengthen the U.S. resolve.	X	
The Weather	**What external conditions will affect operations, and whom do they favor?** Given the tendency of Americans to want things done yesterday, it is unlikely that the population has the patience to sustain a long-term, low-intensity conflict. It is equally unlikely that the United States can quickly defeat al Qaeda. If the U.S. population supports the war effort over time, the United States will certainly prevail. At the moment this scenario seems unlikely, unless al Qaeda makes some serious errors.		X
The Terrain	**Which side is better positioned to take advantage of the environment?** The ability to strike at undefended targets gives the terrorists the ability to inflict physical and psychological harm while disrupting infrastructure and causing divisions among the people and political leaders.		X
Leadership	**Which side has the more capable leadership?** The United States has a breadth and depth of leadership that stretches from line-level officers all the way to the top echelon positions. Al Qaeda has significantly fewer available resources to train and develop leaders. As a result, the United States holds a significant advantage in leadership.	X	
Discipline	**Which side has a clearer system of rewards and punishments?** Overall, the United States enjoys an advantage in possessing a greater number of disciplined forces.	X	

Job Aid 12-6: Criteria for an al Qaeda Victory in the War on Terror

In order for al Qaeda to be victorious it must:

1. Not be destroyed

2. Continue to mount periodic attacks against soft targets

3. Cause division within Western nations via the psychological results of high casualties, spreading fear and creating the accompanying economic disruption

4. Convince the Western populace that the war is not in their interest, thus forcing the withdrawal of Western powers from the world stage

Job Aid 12-7: Criteria for a U.S. Victory in the War on Terror

> In order for the United States and its allies to be victorious they must:
>
> 1. Destroy al Qaeda or neutralize the threat caused by al Qaeda.
>
> 2. Prevent or significantly mitigate the most devastating attacks against the homeland.
>
> 3. Change the mind-set of the American people so that they will understand and support the war on al Qaeda.

Job Aid 12-8: Conclusions: Predictions Regarding the Effort to "Win" the War on Terror

1. The United States and its allies will eventually defeat al Qaeda.

2. Other terror groups will arise over time.

3. As advances in technology continue, the threat posed by terrorist organizations as well as individuals will increase.

4. These same advances in technology will make governments more efficient at ferreting out and destroying terrorist organizations.

5. Concepts of individual liberty will drastically change as societies exchange some of their freedom for security.

Job Aid 12-9: Selected Sun Tzu Quotes

"For to win one hundred victories in one hundred battles is not the acme of skill. To subdue the enemy without fighting is the acme of skill." (Translated by Griffith) (p. 77)

"The Way means inducing the people to have the same aim as the leadership, so that they will share death and share life, without fear of danger." (Translated by Cleary) (p. 2)

"Warfare is the greatest affair of the state, the basis of life and death, the Way (Tao) to survival or extinction. It must be thoroughly pondered and analyzed." (Translated by Sawyer) (p. 167)

"If you know others and know yourself, you will not be imperiled in a hundred battles." (Translated by Cleary) (p. 24)

"The one who figures on victory at headquarters before even doing battle is the one with the most strategic factors on his side. The one who figures on inability to prevail at headquarters before doing battle is the one who has the least strategic factors on his side. The one with many strategic factors in his favor wins, the one with few strategic factors in his favor loses—how much more so for the one with no strategic factors in his favor. Observing this matter in this way, I can see who will win and who will lose." (Translated by Cleary) (pp. 9–10)

"So the important thing in a military operation is victory, not persistence." (Translated by Cleary) (p. 16)

"The superior militarist strikes while schemes are being laid. The next best is to attack alliances. The next best is to attack the army. The lowest is to attack a city. Siege a city only as a last resort." (Translated by Cleary) (p. 18)

"The terrain is to be assessed in terms of distance, difficulty or ease of travel, dimension, and safety." (Translated by Cleary) (p. 3)

"The unorthodox and the orthodox give rise to each other, like a beginningless circle—who could exhaust them?" (Translated by Cleary) (p. 35)

"A military operation involves deception. Even though you are competent, appear to be incompetent. Though effective, appear to be ineffective." (Translated by Cleary) (p. 6)

"Foreknowledge cannot be gotten from ghosts and spirits, cannot be had by analogy, cannot be found out by calculation. It must be obtained from people, people who know the conditions of the enemy." (Translated by Cleary) (p. 111)

"A victorious army first wins and then seeks battle. A defeated army first battles and then seeks victory." (Translated by Cleary) (p. 29)

Annotated Bibliography

1. ASIS International. www.asisonline.org/toolkit/toolkit.xml

   - ASIS International is the world's leading professional association for security specialists. The link noted above has a wide variety of practical information for security professionals.

2. ASIS International. *General Security Risk Assessment Guidelines.* Alexandria, Virginia, 2003.

   - ASIS guidelines in risk assessment and other areas of the security field have gained wide recognition and respect.

3. Baron, Anthony. *Violence in the Workplace: A Prevention and Management Guide for Businesses.* Oxnard, CA: Pathfinder Publishing of California, 1993.

   - An excellent primer on the problem of workplace violence.

4. Cartledge, Paul. *Thermopylae: The Battle That Changed the World.* Woodstock, NY: Overlook Press, Peter Mayer Publishers, 2006.

   - A scholarly, yet highly readable, work that details the battle of Thermopylae, and the ancient world as well.

5. Haddow, George D., and Bullock, Jane A. *Introduction to Emergency Management*, Second Edition. Burlington, MA: Elsevier Butterworth Heinemann, 2006.

   - An outstanding overview of emergency management in the post–9/11 era.

6. *MIPT Terrorist Knowledge Base.* www.tkb.org/Home.jsp

   - In-depth database of terrorist activities and organizations throughout the world. A must for anyone seriously conducting research on terrorism.

7. New York State Metropolitan Transportation Authority. *Field Information—Seven Signs of Terrorist Activity.*

   ▪ A public service announcement distributed to businesses throughout the state of New York. The document briefly outlines signs of potential terrorist activity.

8. Nolan, John A. III, *A Study in French Espionage: Renaissance Software www.hanford.gov/oci/maindocs/ci_r_docs/frenchesp.pdf.* Phoenix Consulting Group; U.S. Department of Energy Website October 2003.

   ▪ An interesting case study on a French espionage operation within the United States.

9. Plutarch. *On Sparta Revised Edition.* Translated by Richard J. A. Talbert, Ian Scott-Kilvert. London, England. Penguin Books, 2005.

   ▪ A classic read for anyone interested in ancient Greek History

10. *Random House Webster's Dictionary*—Third Edition. New York: Ballantine Publishing Group. 1998.

    ▪ A basic dictionary.

11. Rodenbough, Theo, Lanier, Robert S., and Elson, Henry W. (Eds.). *The Photographic History of the Civil War, Three Volumes in One, Armies & Leaders, The Calvary, Decisive Battles.* New York: Portland House, 1997.

    ▪ Information in Chapter 2 on the battle of Manassas Junction/First Bull Run came from this book. This source contains a wealth of well-researched information on the American Civil War and is a must read for any military history buff.

12. Sulzberger, C. L., and The Editors of American Heritage, The Magazine of History. David G. McCullough, Editor in Charge, Ralph K. Andrist, Pictorial Commentary. *The American Heritage Picture History of World War II.* New York: Heritage Publishing Company, Inc. 1966.

    ▪ This source on the Second World War is well researched and contains hundreds of excellent period photographs.

13. Tzu, Sun. *The Art of War.* Translated by Thomas Cleary. Boston: Shambhala Publications, 1991.

    ▪ This version of *The Art of War* is short, easy to read, and contains commentary.

14. Tzu, Sun. *The Art of War.* Translated by Samuel Griffith. London: Oxford University Press, 1963.

   - A classic interpretation. This version of *The Art of War* is exceptionally well researched, easy to read, and contains a wealth of information on both the original text and the ancient history of China.

15. Tzu, Sun. *The Art of War.* Translated by Ralph D. Sawyer. Boulder, CO: Westview Press, 1994.

   - This version of *The Art of War* is very scholarly, yet still maintains a readability that is rare among academic authors. The work is full of historical information on ancient China.

16. Tzu, Sun. *The Art of War for Managers; 50 Strategic Rules.* Interpreted by Gerald A. Michaelson. Avon, MA: Adams Media Corporation, 2001.

   - *The Art of War for Managers* takes 50 lessons from Sun Tzu's classic and applies them, with great success, to the corporate world.

17. *The 9/11 Commission Report.* www.9-11commission.gov/report/911Report.pdf

   - An in-depth examination of the events leading up to the September 11, 2001 attacks upon the United States.

Index

CPSIA information can be obtained
at www.ICGtesting.com
Printed in the USA
LVHW080523091019
633667LV00011B/125/P